THE ORTHO

MW01136600

SHEPHERDING THE FLOCK

THE PASTORAL EPISTLES OF ST. PAUL THE APOSTLE TO TIMOTHY AND TO TITUS

by Fr. Lawrence R. Farley

Ancient Faith Publishing
Chesterton, Indiana

SHEPHERDING THE FLOCK:
THE PASTORAL EPISTLES OF ST. PAUL THE APOSTLE
TO TIMOTHY AND TO TITUS
© Copyright 2007 by Lawrence Farley

One volume of *The Orthodox Bible Study Companion Series*

Published by   Ancient Faith Publishing
               A division of Ancient Faith Ministries
               P.O. Box 748
               Chesterton, IN 46304

ISBN 978-1-888212-56-3

Printed in the United States of America

30 29 28 27 26 25 24 23 22 21 20   7 6 5 4 3

Dedicated to those early friends who led me to Jesus:
Dianne, Steve and Charlie

Table of Contents and Outline

St. Paul's Epistle to Titus

St. Paul's Second Epistle to Timothy

Excurses:

❧ Introduction ☙

A Word about Scholarship and Translation

This commentary was written for your grandmother. And for your plumber, your banker, your next-door neighbor, and the girl who serves you French fries at the nearby McDonald's. That is, it was written for the average layman, for the nonprofessional who feels a bit intimidated by the presence of copious footnotes, long bibliographies, and all those other things which so enrich the lives of academics. It is written for the pious Orthodox layman who is mystified by such things as Source Criticism, but who nonetheless wants to know what the Scriptures mean.

Therefore, it is unlike many other commentaries, which are written as contributions to the ongoing endeavor of scholarship and as parts of a continuous dialogue among scholars. That endeavor and dialogue is indeed worthwhile, but the present commentary forms no part of it. For it assumes, without argument, a certain point of view, and asserts it without defense, believing it to be consistent with the presuppositions of the Fathers and therefore consistent with Orthodox Tradition. It has but one aim: to be the sort of book a busy parish priest might put in the hands of an interested parishioner who says to him over coffee hour after Liturgy, "Father, I'm not sure I really get what St. Paul is saying in the Epistles. What does it all mean?" This commentary tries to tell the perplexed parishioner what the writers of the New Testament mean.

Regarding the translation used herein, an Italian proverb says, "All translators are traitors." (The proverb proves its own point, for it sounds better in Italian!) The point of the proverb, of course, is that no translation, however careful, can bring out all the nuances and meanings of the original, since no language can be the mathematical equivalent of another. The English translator is faced, it would seem, with a choice: either he can make the translation something of a rough paraphrase of the original and render it into flowing sonorous English; or he can attempt to make a fairly literal, word-for-word translation from the original with the resultant English being stilted, wooden, and clumsy.

These two basic and different approaches to translation correspond to two basic and different activities in the Church. The Church needs a translation of the Scriptures for use in worship. This should be in good, grammatical, and flowing English, as elegant as possible and suited to its function in the majestic worship of the Liturgy. The Church also needs a translation of the Scriptures for private study and for group Bible study. Here the elegance of its English is of lesser concern. What is of greater concern here is the bringing out of all the nuances found in the original. Thus this approach will tend to sacrifice elegance for literality and, wherever possible, seek a word-for-word correspondence with the Greek. Also, because the student will want to see how the biblical authors use a particular word (especially St. Paul, who has many works included in the canon), a consistency of translation will be sought and the same Greek word will be translated, wherever possible, by the same English word or by its cognate.

The present work does not pretend to be anything other than a translation for private Bible study. It seeks to achieve, as much as possible, a literal, word-for-word correspondence with the Greek. The aim has been to present a translation from which one could jump back into the Greek original with the aid of an interlinear New Testament. Where a single Greek word has been used in the original, I have tried to find (or invent!) a single English word.

The result, of course, is a translation so literally rendered from the Greek that it represents an English spoken nowhere on the planet! That is, it represents a kind of "study Bible English" and not an actual vernacular. It was never intended for use outside the present commentaries, much less in the worship of the Church. The task of producing a flowing, elegant translation that nonetheless preserves the integrity and nuances of the original I cheerfully leave to hands more competent than mine.

The Pastoral Epistles

"And what happened next? How does the story end?" All parents hear this wide-eyed cry from their young children when they conclude one chapter of a continuing story and close the book for the night—so long as it is a story, of course, whose protagonist has captured the heart of the child.

The difficulty of answering these questions attends the story of St. Paul, especially in commenting on his epistles to Timothy and to Titus. We can follow the early chapters of his story in its broad outlines without too much difficulty by inserting his epistles into the narrative of St. Luke's *Acts of the Apostles*. That story ends with St. Paul in a Roman prison awaiting trial. (We may conclude, as did the Fathers, that the trial ended with his acquittal and release.) The question remains, "What happened next?" Where did St. Paul go after that? How does his story end, and what is the way he took that led him at last to rearrest and his final trial and martyrdom?

We can glean some insight from the incidental geographical details in the Pastoral Epistles themselves. The difficulty is to piece them together into an actual itinerary. Many scholars have done this, each coming up with a different route. This in itself is proof of the difficulty of the task, and any reconstruction of St. Paul's journeys after his release from his first imprisonment must remain conjectural. Nonetheless, I offer the following.

Paul was (as the Fathers assert) acquitted at his first imprisonment and trial, which occurred in (perhaps) AD 62. Where did he go then? Again, scholars are of different minds. But we may ask, "Where would *you* go after release from prison?" In fact, where would anyone go? I would suggest that we can sum up the obvious destination in one precious word: Home. After a long imprisonment lasting more than two years (Acts 28:30), the apostle started home to Antioch, the place from which he set out on his journeys and to which he returned after them. Crete was on the way, and I suggest that he made a quick tour there en route, leaving his traveling companion Titus there to finish up (see Titus 1:5). From Antioch, he set out again, reaching Asia by the summer. He had promised Philemon of Colossae that he would return to visit him (Philemon

22), and we know that he visited Ephesus too, for he left Timothy there (1 Tim. 1:3). (Did Timothy also accompany Paul all the way from his release in Rome?)

After a time in Asia, Paul may well have crossed to Macedonia, for he had promised the Philippians there that he would visit them again (Phil. 2:24). It was, I suggest, from Philippi that he wrote his First Epistle to Timothy, as his young companion waited in Ephesus. Also, he wrote his Epistle to Titus as he continued his work in Crete, sending it to him by the hand of Zenas and Apollos (Titus 3:13). Paul hoped to send Artemas or Tychicus to Crete later; when these came to take Titus' place there, Titus himself was to leave to join Paul in Nicopolis for the winter (Titus 3:12–13). We may think, then, that Paul fulfilled this plan, stayed in Nicopolis for that autumn, and was joined there by Titus.

What happened then? The Fathers are emphatic that Paul fulfilled his long-held plan to visit Spain (see Rom. 15:24), and we may date this trip perhaps to this time. (This assumes that he actually fulfilled this desire. It could be that the Fathers' view that he visited Spain was simply a deduction from Paul's stated intention in Romans 15:24 and that Paul never did make it to Spain. On the other hand, Paul was not a man whose longstanding desires were easily put off!) His trip to Spain would then have occupied the spring of 63, allowing him to return after a year or two's work in the spring of 65.

St. Paul may well have done much work not recorded in the Pastoral Epistles. We know that he was in Troas (see 2 Tim. 4:13). I would suggest that he was arrested again when he revisited Ephesus (possibly in the spring of 65), and this arrest was responsible for Timothy's tears mentioned in 2 Tim. 1:4. (It may well have been this arrest which caused all those in Asia, formerly his supporters, to desert him out of concern for their own safety; 2 Tim. 1:15.) Paul was then taken to Rome for his second and final imprisonment, traveling by way of Miletus (2 Tim. 4:20). He was in Rome by the summer of 65.

He had a preliminary hearing, I suggest (2 Tim. 4:16), after which Onesiphorus tracked him down and befriended him (2 Tim. 1:16, 17). (Onesiphorus later died, though in what circumstances it remains impossible to guess.) Paul sent Tychicus to Timothy in Ephesus (2 Tim. 4:12). Later, possibly in the late summer or early autumn of 65, Paul wrote his Second Epistle to Timothy, urging him to come to him in Rome. Paul languished in prison all that winter, and was finally martyred by beheading at the end of June 66.

All of this, of course, remains conjecture, both regarding the itinerary and activities of Paul and regarding the timing. What remains certain, however, is that he did visit these places mentioned in his epistles before being rearrested and martyred in Rome under Nero.

What then is the abiding significance of these epistles? Scholars have called them the Pastoral Epistles since they deal with pastoral matters, instructing Timothy and Titus how to shepherd the flock of God scattered throughout the world. The geographical and autobiographical details remain incidental. More important is Paul's teaching about "how one ought to conduct oneself in the House of God," the Church (1 Tim. 3:15). As a loving shepherd, charged by Christ the Archshepherd to care for the souls of men committed to him, St. Paul takes care to instruct others to shepherd the flock as well, and the wisdom born from such pastoral and loving care makes these epistles timeless and precious. We, like children hearing a story, care about what happened to the writer. His final three epistles remain as a testimony to his pastoral love and as an inspiration for those in the Church, both the shepherds and the flock, to walk in holiness and love themselves.

Key to the Format of This Work:

• The translated text is first presented in boldface type. Italics within these biblical text sections represent words required by English syntax that are not actually present in the Greek. Each translated text section is set within a shaded grey box.

ॐ ॐ ॐ ॐ ॐ

18 **This order I commit to you, Timothy my child, according to the previously-given prophecies about you, that by them you may fight the good fight,**

19 **holding faith and a good conscience, which some have pushed-aside and made shipwreck of the Faith,**

• In the commentary sections, citations from the portion of text being commented upon are given in boldface type.

Paul therefore recalls the **previously-given prophecies** made about Timothy, probably at the time of his ordination.

• In the commentary sections, citations from other locations in Scripture are given in quotation marks with a reference; any reference not including a book name refers to the book under discussion.

"Faith" refers here to the fruit of the Spirit of tenacious faithfulness (Gal. 5:22)

• In the commentary sections, italics are used in the ordinary way—for emphasis, foreign words, etc.

On that occasion, the eldership or assembly of elders (Gr. *presbuteros* or presbyters) laid their hands on Timothy, invoking God's Spirit.

❧ St. Paul's First Epistle to Timothy ❧

Introduction

When Paul left Timothy in Ephesus (1:3), he must have known what a weight he was placing on Timothy's comparatively youthful shoulders. Ephesus was a huge city, the key to success in Asia Minor, and Paul knew it was crucial that the Christian work there prosper.

Not only that, Timothy had to face many challenges as he shepherded the church in Ephesus. The city teemed with religions and with many religious self-promoters, spiritual hucksters, all eager to pass themselves off as teachers of deeper truths to those seeking enlightenment. These influences threatened the purity of the Gospel and had to be resisted at all costs. Of special concern to Paul were those propagating "Jewish myths" (1:3–4; 4:7): the Jewish component in their teaching might appeal to Christians, who knew themselves to be part of "the commonwealth of Israel" (Eph. 2:12). These men had already become part of the Church, though they had little concern for conscience, practical piety, or holiness. They did, however, delight in being thought teachers (1:7) and were pushing to have themselves ordained to the office of bishop/presbyter in the Church, or at least to the diaconate. They looked down on Timothy, who was younger than they (4:12). Paul told Timothy to concentrate on the teaching of true doctrine and to counteract their influence (4:13–14).

What was the nature of these "Jewish myths"? It is difficult to know for certain, but it seems that they were highly allegorical. Some echoes of this kind of teaching may survive in the Jewish Book of Jubilees, which recounts stories of the Law, including long genealogies (1:4).

Paul found other problems affecting the Ephesian church as well. The Christians there had a tendency to quarrel, resulting in dissension (2:8). The women were overstepping their boundaries, desiring to be teachers of the law and rulers within the church (2:9). Moreover, the church had trouble with the widows. These widows were not merely women who had been bereaved of their husbands, but women who had been placed on an official list as church widows. In return for support, these women had pledged themselves to lives of singleness and prayer. Some of the younger of them, despite their pledge, had chosen to remarry (5:11). The church was thus in danger of being discredited by their idleness and self-indulgence (5:6), and Timothy needed to attend to this danger as well. Further, the wealthy were reluctant to share their wealth with their Christian brothers (6:17–19), which perhaps contributed even more to the dissension and resentment that threatened the church's unity. In short, Timothy needed to take careful oversight of the many and varied relationships existing in the church with a pastoral eye to preserving good order (3:15).

St. Paul wrote this first epistle to his young friend to help him fulfill his challenging task as he labored for Christ in the great city of Ephesus. We may date the epistle around the summer of AD 62, sent from Macedonia.

❧ The First Epistle
of St. Paul the Apostle to Timothy ❧

§I. Opening Greetings (1:1, 2)

> ❧ ❧ ❧ ❧ ❧
>
> **1** 1 Paul, an apostle of Christ Jesus according to
>   the command of God our Savior and of Christ
>   Jesus our hope;
>   2 to Timothy, my genuine child in *the* Faith:
>   grace, mercy, and peace from God the Father
>   and Christ Jesus our Lord.

Though this epistle is sent **to Timothy**, Paul is aware that it will be read by those in Ephesus over whom Timothy has been given charge, and therefore it is sent as a kind of open letter to them as well. That is, it is sent not simply to instruct Timothy regarding his duties, but also as proof of his apostolic authorization to perform them. That is why Paul stresses his apostolic authority in the opening verse. Usually, he refers to this authority by saying that he was made an apostle "by the will of God" (see for example 1 Cor. 1:1; Eph. 1:1; Col. 1:1). Here, however, he uses the stronger phrase **according to the command of God**, and by so doing emphasizes his authority. He expects this authority, conferred upon Timothy by the instructions in this epistle, to be respected and obeyed. For Timothy is not simply another one of Paul's co-workers. He is more than that—he is his **genuine child in *the* Faith**, and Paul wants those in Ephesus to know that to disregard Timothy would be to disregard himself as well.

Paul describes **God** as **our Savior**. That is, God has acted decisively to save the world through the work of **Christ Jesus**. God does not simply sit passively in the heavens and superintend the world's order; as the Lover of mankind, He actively works for the redemption of the world He made, working salvation in the midst of the earth through Jesus of Nazareth. Paul describes Jesus as **our hope**, because discipleship to Him will lead ultimately to life in the age to come. Our culture uses the word "hope" in a mild, rather uncertain sense: one "hopes" to win the lottery, but has no certainty of it. When Paul uses the word "hope" (Gr. *elpis*), he intends something strong and sure. "Hope" in the Pauline vocabulary is an anchor that keeps us from drifting, a rock to build on. In describing Christ Jesus as "our hope," Paul means that the future is filled with the certitude of joy for Christ's people, so long as they cling to their allegiance to Christ.

Paul's greeting to Timothy is different from his other epistolary greetings. Usually Paul greets those to whom he writes simply by bidding them **grace** and **peace**, but here he adds a wish for God's **mercy** on his spiritual child as well. Paul is only too aware of the magnitude of the task facing his young friend, and he prays for a special mercy of protection.

In all of Paul's epistles, we note too how closely **Christ Jesus** is associated with **God the Father**, since They share the same indivisible Godhead. Paul's apostolate derives from Their joint command, and the grace, mercy, and peace he prays for Timothy come from both as well, as from one Source.

§II.   The Need at Ephesus:
Timothy to Resist Strange Teachings (1:3–11)

ॐ ॐ ॐ ॐ ॐ

3   As I urged you while I was going into Macedonia, remain on at Ephesus that you may order certain ones not to teach other *doctrines*,

4   nor to pay attention to myths and endless

> genealogies, which cause speculations rather than the stewardship of God which is in faith.
>
> 5 But the end of the order *we give* is love from a clean heart and a good conscience and an unhypocritical faith,
>
> 6 from which things some have missed *the mark* and turned aside to useless-talk,
>
> 7 wanting to be teachers of the Law, though they do not understand either what they say or the things they insist upon.

Paul repeats the main purpose of his letter: to encourage Timothy to counteract the spread of harmful false teaching in Ephesus. He previously told him this when he **was going into Macedonia** and leaving his protégé behind to **remain on at Ephesus**. Doubtless Timothy wanted to accompany Paul, but Paul told him that it was necessary for him to stay where he was and ensure that the apostolic doctrine preached was not subverted. Though Paul gave this charge orally to Timothy before he left, he gives it to him again, putting it down in writing so that any who question Timothy's mandate may read it for themselves. Specifically, Timothy is to **order certain ones not to teach** heterodoxy, **other *doctrines*** than were laid down by the apostles (Gr. *eterodidaskaleo*, lit., "to teach other things"). These *certain ones* are perhaps known, but left unnamed, for Paul means to throw the net as widely as possible. It matters not who they are—let no one teach strange things!

What are these *other doctrines*? Paul further describes them as a preoccupation with **myths and endless genealogies**. We may find an example of such Jewish works in the "Book of Jubilees," which recounts stories from the Law (including the genealogies), investing them with deeper allegorical meanings. These works were simply exercises in subjectivity and tended only to **speculations** and mental games. They had no practical significance for the lives of believers. The Gospel **stewardship of God** administered by the apostles, on the other hand, which consists of **faith** in Jesus, *does* have practical significance. The **end** and goal of **the order** Timothy will give is **love from a clean heart and a good conscience and an unhypocritical faith**.

Here we see the essentially transformative nature of the Christian Faith. Doctrine and liturgy are not self-contained ends in themselves, but rather the means to a transformed life. Religion that does not alter a person's life for the good, making him more loving, more responsive to the demands of conscience, and more sincere, is not true religion at all. True religion resides in the heart, and from there radiates outward in the form of good works. A religion confined to the head and manifest only in religious rituals is no better than idle speculation.

Paul needs to stress these things because the teachings promoted by these men have no such transformative component. They **have missed** *the mark*, wandering from the main path of apostolic doctrine, and **turned aside** into tangled footpaths and dead ends. They end up mired in **useless-talk** (Gr. *matailogia*, idiomatically rendered as "jive-talk"). It all sounds great but has no relation to reality. These men want to be **teachers of the Law**; they crave the esteem that comes with a reputation for deep philosophical wisdom. Though desperate to appear profound, they actually do **not understand either what they say**, nor the implications of **the things they insist upon**. They delight in using the Law as fodder for their allegorical meanings and pretend to draw out its deeper, hidden significance. The Law, they proclaim, can lead one to full maturity, as that which contains all the treasures of wisdom and knowledge (see Col. 2:2–3 for the true source of wisdom and knowledge). They say that one need only **pay attention to** and dwell upon the Law to plumb the secret depths of divine knowledge (with their assistance, of course!).

ॐ ॐ ॐ ॐ ॐ

8   Now we know that the Law *is* good, if one uses
    it lawfully,

9   knowing this, that law is not laid down for
    a righteous *person*, but for *the* lawless and
    insubordinate, *for* impious and sinners, *for*

> the unholy and profane, *for* father-killers and
> mother-killers, for murderers,
> 10 fornicators, homosexuals, kidnappers, liars,
> perjurers, and whatever else is contrary to
> healthy teaching,
> 11 according to the glorious Gospel of the blessed
> God with which I have been entrusted.

Contrary to this, St. Paul reveals the true and proper use of the Jewish Law. God did not give Israel the Law to lead them to maturity and transforming holiness; only Christ, the end and goal of the Law, can do that (see Rom. 10:4). The **Law** (Gr. *nomos*) is indeed **good** and useful—but only **if one uses it lawfully** (Gr. *nomimos*) and in accordance with its true nature. God did not create the Law for good men, to help them reach the final goal of holiness and the Kingdom. It was **not laid down for a righteous *person***, such as these teachers all claim to be. Rather, any law was obviously given **for *the* lawless and insubordinate** persons who would otherwise throw off all restraint. That was the point of all those prohibitions. For why tell a righteous man that he must not kill his father? He has no desire to do so. The Law was manifestly given for all kinds of unrighteous persons, for the worst sort—and here Paul gives an extensive list of different types of sinners. By forbidding such behaviors and laying down penalties for them, the Law shows that it was given for these sorts of people—or at least for those tempted to do those things.

The list of sinners is not meant to be exhaustive, but merely illustrative of the depths of sin which the Law is meant to restrain. **Impious and sinners** are general designations for those who take no care for religion and righteous living. **Unholy and profane** indicate likewise those who trample on the decencies of life, both natural and religious. **Father-killers and mother-killers** indicate those who rise up in anger to slay their parents, thus violating the earliest and most basic demands of gratitude by killing those who first gave them life.

St. Paul then piles up word upon word, sin upon sin. The

connecting "ands" fall away from the list—the first eight words come in pairs, but now as Paul plunges deeper into his task, words tumble out quickly and heatedly, one after another, in an unbroken list of depravities. He speaks of **murderers** (lit. "manslayers," denoting murder of all kinds). He lists **fornicators** (those who have sexual relations outside marriage) and **homosexuals** (men who indulge in sexual acts with other men). He speaks of **kidnappers** (those who kidnap others to sell as slaves) and **liars** of all kinds, **perjurers** who even lie under oath. Unwilling to plunge further into the pit, he sums up all the rest as **whatever else is contrary to healthy teaching**.

Those preoccupied with such "Jewish myths" and such a use of the Law claim that the Law can produce spiritual health. On the contrary, says Paul, the Law was given to restrain those who *resist* healthy teaching! Humanity can only find such spiritual health in **the glorious Gospel of the blessed God with which** he, Paul, has been **entrusted**.

§III.   Opening Thanksgiving (1:12–17)

༄ ༄ ༄ ༄ ༄

12 I thank Christ Jesus our Lord, who empowered me, because He esteemed me faithful, putting *me* into service,

13 *though* I was formerly a blasphemer and a persecutor and an abusive *man.* But I *received* mercy because I did *it* ignorantly in faithlessness,

14 and the grace of our Lord superabounded with the faith and love *that are* in Christ Jesus.

15 Faithful *is* the word, and worthy of all acceptance, that Christ Jesus came into the world to save sinners, of whom I *myself* am first.

16 But because of this I *received* mercy, that in me *as* first, Jesus Christ might demonstrate *the* whole *of* His patience as a model for those

> who would later have faith in Him for eternal
> life.
> 17 Now to the King of the ages, incorruptible,
> invisible, *the* only God, *be* honor and glory to
> the ages of the ages! Amen.

After his opening broadside at those Timothy must oppose, St. Paul proceeds to the opening epistolary thanksgiving characteristic of his epistles (compare 1 Cor. 1:4f; Phil. 1:3f; Col. 1:3f). He is grateful to **Christ Jesus** for the mercy that he himself received from Him. Mention (in v. 11) of the glorious Gospel with which he has been entrusted (Gr. *pisteuo*) makes him reflect again how miraculous it is that he has been so entrusted. Christ indeed considered him **faithful** (or trustworthy, Gr. *pistos*—a play on words with "entrusted," v. 11) and **empowered** him with His Spirit (see 9:17), **putting** him **into service** as His apostolic servant.

Paul never forgot the sin, guilt, and darkness from which His Lord had saved him, nor the overwhelming grace and unmerited favor showered upon him when Christ called him. When Christ arrested Paul's headlong progress on the road to Damascus (Acts 9), he was no servant of His. Rather, he was **a blasphemer and a persecutor and an abusive *man***, abusing and beating Christ's humble servants, deserving only judgment and divine wrath. How could such a one be **esteemed** faithful and worth the risk of being entrusted with such an important task? Simply because he had acted **ignorantly in faithlessness**. That is, his faithlessness was not the result of sinning against his conscience. Paul had not hardened his heart, turning away from what he knew was the truth. Rather, he persecuted the Church ignorantly, in good conscience, misguidedly thinking he was serving God. This did not make his persecution any less a sin, but it did mean that the way of repentance still lay wide open to him. Because he had not hardened his heart, he could turn the more easily to follow the truth when it was revealed to him. So it was that he *received* **mercy** on the road to Damascus and was "put into service" as the Lord's apostle, entrusted with His Gospel. The **grace of our Lord superabounded** and overflowed, bearing much fruit in his life, even **the faith** (or faithfulness) **and love** *that are* **in Christ Jesus**, fruitfulness that is available to anyone in the Church.

St. Paul then quotes a **faithful word** or saying (perhaps a proverb current in the Church) that he commends as **worthy of all acceptance**, whose truth may be relied upon by all: **Christ Jesus came into the world to save sinners**. That is, Christ came not simply to reward the righteous, but to restore, heal, and save even the notoriously irreligious, the sinners (the verb "save" is the Gr. *sozo*; compare its use in Mark 5:34). He came to gather into His Kingdom all the children of men, including the tax collectors and prostitutes—even blasphemers and persecutors. Among such sinners, Paul feels himself to be **first** and foremost. (Such is the saving work of the conscience: every man, when ashamed of his sin, feels himself worse than all, ready to run to God in repentance.)

That is why, Paul reasons, he *received mercy*. As *first* among sinners and notorious for his persecution of the Church, he could provide the perfect paradigm and be **a model for those who would later have faith** in Jesus. In Paul's case, **Jesus Christ** could **demonstrate** *the* **whole** *of* **His patience**. The mercy shown to Paul the persecutor revealed that mercy can be obtained by *any* who will come to Jesus. If Paul could return to Christ and find such acceptance, there is no one who is beyond saving. Paul's conversion and apostolate remain as a beacon for the lost, a summons for all the sinners to come home and find a welcome. In saving Paul the prodigal, Christ opened His heart and displayed His boundless compassion for all sinners everywhere.

This demonstration of mercy fills Paul's heart as he begins his epistle to Timothy—that our salvation is not in the Law, but in the boundless mercy of Jesus. Thinking of this, he bursts out in a liturgical cry of praise to the God of Israel, who through His Christ gave such mercy to the world: **Now to the King of the ages, incorruptible, invisible,** *the* **only God,** *be* **honor and glory to the ages of the ages! Amen.** God is utterly transcendent—not subject to corruption and mortality, not able to be apprehended by the eyes of men, alone exalted and utterly without peer. Yet this transcendent God reached down to save us, performing great exploits in His Christ to find and rescue the lost sheep—even a sheep as lost as Paul the persecutor. No wonder Paul cries out with such an exclamation, ascribing to Him eternal honor and glory!

§IV.   Timothy to Receive Paul's Order (1:18–20)

ॐ ॐ ॐ ॐ ॐ

18 This order I commit to you, Timothy my child, according to the previously-given prophecies about you, that by them you may fight the good fight,

19 holding faith and a good conscience, which some have pushed-aside and made shipwreck of the Faith,

20 among whom are Hymenaeus and Alexander, whom I have delivered *up* to Satan that they may be disciplined not to blaspheme.

Paul then speaks from the heart to **Timothy** his true **child**, with personal words of encouragement and advice—something he does a number of times in this epistle (3:14–16; 4:6–16; 6:11–16, 20–21), making this not just an open letter, but also a warm appeal of a father to his spiritual child. In addressing Timothy not just as his son but as his child, Paul opens his heart to him, speaking with great tenderness; he knows the daunting size of the task facing his young protégé. To encourage him in this task, Paul solemnly **commits** and entrusts him with this **order** or charge (compare 1:5) to teach the truth, regardless of the opposition. Timothy needs not only compassion, but also steel in his soul and the courage to stare down the opposition.

Paul therefore recalls the **previously-given prophecies** made about Timothy, probably at the time of his ordination. On that occasion, the eldership or assembly of elders (Gr. *presbuteros* or presbyters) laid their hands on Timothy, invoking God's Spirit with His manifold *charismata* or gifts. At this time one of them prophesied (4:14)—probably in general terms about how God was calling Timothy to this important work (compare a similar prophecy regarding Paul and Barnabas in Acts 13:2). When challenges multiply and the task at hand seems greater than he can perform, Timothy is to remember these prophecies and rely not on his own power but on the strength of God. It is with this support that he can **fight the good fight**. If Timothy relies on his own strength, he will fail. Paul urges the young man to look beyond his own resources to the boundless power of God. In the dark night of despair, Timothy is to recall these prophetic words and find in them the light to battle on.

The words for "fight" (Gr. *strateuo, strateia*) mean literally to fight as a soldier in the army; they are echoes not of the boxing ring, but of the battlefield. Christ has made Timothy His soldier, and he should expect the same hardship and hazards that soldiers endure while on the frontline. But Timothy is not fighting an ignoble battle waged for selfish nationalistic ends. It is a good war, waged by God against the spiritual forces of evil, and one that Timothy can commit himself to with all his heart.

To be victorious, however, he must **hold** fast to **faith**. "Faith" refers here to the fruit of the Spirit of tenacious faithfulness (Gal. 5:22), a determination to persevere in God's service, never counting the cost, never heeding the wounds. No matter how dark things become, no matter how badly the warfare goes, no matter how overwhelming the hosts arrayed against him, there must be no retreat, no surrender. He must believe in the rightness of his cause no matter what. Paul couples this persevering faithfulness with **a good conscience**, a sensitivity to the dictates of the inner moral compass. The enemy will certainly tempt Timothy—as he does all Christian young men—with all kinds of temptations, including sexual ones. To avoid being a casualty in the spiritual warfare in which he is engaged, Timothy must stay clean. His opposition has no real place for such things in their preoccupation with myths (1:4–6), but Timothy is to keep moral rectitude front and center. Some have **pushed-aside** and repudiated conscience as irrelevant, only to **make shipwreck** of that **Faith** they once held. Timothy must learn from their examples and not follow them to disaster.

St. Paul then mentions two such shipwrecked persons by name:

Hymenaeus and Alexander. In singling them out for special mention, Paul is not concerned to further hold them up to shame. Rather, Paul wants to warn Timothy (and those of his flock reading Paul's open letter over Timothy's shoulder) not to receive these two into communion. Paul excommunicated them before leaving Ephesus, **delivering *up*** the pair **to Satan**. This excommunication must be heeded and upheld!

The phrase "delivered up to Satan" reveals that the Church is a haven of sanctuary and safety, the one place in the world where Satan's power has been neutralized. The Church is an island of light in a world of darkness, a place of peace in a cosmos torn by war. Satan reigns in this world as its ruler (John 12:31), but his sovereignty ceases at the doors of the Church. In the Church, only the crucified King, Jesus the Lord of glory, holds sovereign sway. For the Church to disown a former member by excommunicating him (that is, by refusing him Holy Communion at the weekly Eucharist) is to return the erring sinner to the realm where Satan rules (compare 1 John 5:19). This is not simply punitive, however, but that they might be **disciplined** and taught, punished as children are disciplined (Gr. *paideuo*; compare its use in Heb. 12:6–8). Formerly they continued to **blaspheme**. That is, their false teaching is equated with blasphemy, with denouncing the honor of God. Paul hopes that through excommunication, they will be brought to repent of their false teaching and return to the Church, no longer impugning God's honor with their heresy. Meanwhile, Timothy and others are to refuse to receive them.

§V.   Prayer and Order in the Church (2:1–15)

ॐ   ॐ   ॐ   ॐ   ॐ

2 1   I exhort, therefore, first of all, that supplications, prayers, petitions, and thanksgivings be made for all men,

2   for kings and all the ones in prominence, that

> we may lead a tranquil and quiet life in all piety
> and reverence.
> 3 This *is* good and acceptable before God our
>   Savior,
> 4 who wishes all men to be saved and to come to
>   the real-knowledge of *the* Truth.
> 5 For *there is* one God, and one Mediator be-
>   tween God and men, *the* Man Christ Jesus,
> 6 who gave Himself *as* a ransom for all, the wit-
>   ness *of it* in its own times.
> 7 For this I *myself* was appointed a herald and an
>   apostle (I am telling *the* truth, I am not lying),
>   a teacher of the Gentiles in faith and truth.

St. Paul begins to **exhort** Timothy, laying down the direction in which the church under his care should go. Paul connects this exhortation with the charge that preceded it, using the connective particle **therefore** (Gr. *oun*), because obeying the directives that follow is the way in which Timothy will fulfill his charge.

First of all in importance, Paul mentions the necessity to pray for peace in the world so that the Church can carry out its holy work. Though a small and somewhat embattled movement, the Church must not constrict its outlook or limit its focus. It must not shrink defensively into itself like a sect or a cult. Rather, it must have a global outlook and gather the whole world into its embrace. Paul promotes a universal perspective, referring to **all men** four times in these first six verses (vv. 1, 2, 4, 6). As of first importance, the Church must preserve this global generosity of concern.

This universal outlook of Paul's shows his immense vision. At the time Paul wrote, the Christian movement remained a small sect, an increasingly embattled minority struggling for survival in a hostile world. It would have been natural for Paul to adopt a more defensive posture, being concerned "first of all" that the Church simply continue to endure. But, as the saying goes, "The best defense is a good offense." Paul is not concerned with mere survival for the Church, but with her growth and expansion. He refuses to look selfishly inward, but lifts up his gaze and surveys the whole world. Christ shed His Blood for all the world, and the Church must hold in her heart all for whom Christ died.

Thus Paul orders that prayers of all kinds be offered for all public figures, not only for **kings**, but also for **all the ones in prominence**, such as local civic leaders, Roman rulers, and all having social responsibility. The Church must hold all of them up to God in her official intercession at the weekly Eucharist. The Church is to offer **supplications** (Gr. *deesis*), **prayers** (Gr. *proseuche*), **petitions** (Gr. *enteuxis*), and **thanksgivings** (Gr. *eucharistia*) on behalf of all. Though these four different words are used, it is unlikely that Paul has in mind four rigorously differentiated kinds of prayer. His main point seems to be that there is no kind of prayer that should not be offered—let the Church pray well and thoroughly for the peace and stability of the whole world. For when God grants their prayers, the Church will enjoy peace and will be able to **lead a tranquil and quiet life in all piety and reverence**.

It was the same with the Israelites living in exile in Babylon: by seeking for the peace of the pagan society around them, the Jews found God's provision for themselves also (Jer. 29:7). By praying for the pagan world surrounding them, the Church too will receive the peace necessary to preach and live out the Gospel. God wants the Christians to move about in society as persons committed to "tranquil and quiet" lives, not as political firebrands; they are to be distinguished by their "piety and reverence" as irreproachable and contributing members of society, not as potential rebels and troublemakers.

St. Paul insists that this prayer for their pagan rulers is **good and acceptable before God our Savior**. Paul has to insist on this point, for there are many in Ephesus (especially those of Jewish background) who have no love for Roman rule and who would more easily accept God's wrath on their pagan rulers than His love for them. How could it be right, they ask, to pray God's blessing on these idolatrous pagans? St. Paul therefore stresses that even such pagans are not beyond the care of God. God **wishes all men to be saved and to come to the real-knowledge** and experience (Gr. *epignosis*) **of *the* Truth** about Christ. For *there is* **one God** for all men, Gentiles as well as Jews (Rom. 3:29). More than that, there is also **one Mediator between God and men**, a **Man** Himself, even **Christ Jesus**. Men of all kinds, Gentile and Jew alike, may draw near to God through Him. Since God sent Jesus as a "Mediator" (Gr. *mesites*, one who reconciles the previously estranged) for all people, He obviously cares for all people, even the pagans, striving to draw them to repentance and salvation. This being so, it cannot be wrong to pray for those for whom Christ is a Mediator.

In describing Christ as a "Man" (Gr. *anthropos*), St. Paul focuses on the divine dispensation, or plan of salvation, in which the timeless Word became incarnate for our sake. The eternal Word became a Man, and as a Man **gave Himself *as* a ransom for all**—for Gentile as well as Jew. He shed His precious Blood for all to buy back the universe for God, redeeming it from mortality and corruption. St. Paul uses the metaphor of a "ransom" (Gr. *antilutron*) to show how we, who were formerly slaves to death, are now set free. It is pushing his metaphor too far to ask such questions as to whom the ransom was paid. This redeeming death itself forms the definitive **witness** to the love of God and His universal care for all men—which witness came **in its own times** (Gr. *kairois idiois*) and at the eschatological end of the ages (1 Cor. 10:11). This ransom proves once and for all that God desires to embrace and save the world.

Paul insists that this is the whole point of his ministry. He himself (the pronoun is emphatic in the Greek) was appointed as **a herald and an apostle** to proclaim this universal love of God. Some of his opponents deny his apostolic authority, but Paul is God's appointee nonetheless, and he asserts over and over again that he is **telling *the* truth** and **not lying** about it. On the road to Damascus, he was indeed appointed to be **a teacher of the Gentiles**, to instruct them in the **faith** of the Church and the **truth** of the Gospel. Paul's very existence as an apostle testifies of God's concern for all the world, so the Church should not shrink from including the world in its prayerful embrace.

In using the term "teacher of the Gentiles" (or of "the nations"), Paul claims a great dignity, for the term "teacher" (Gr. *didaskalos*) retained great nobility. It is like our present title "Doctor" (which originally meant "teacher," one skilled in doctrine) in that one claiming to be a doctor today receives great respect. Paul claims such respect for himself, saying that God has made him an instructor, model, and benefactor to all the nations. This repeated claim of Paul (see Rom. 1:1; 1 Cor. 1:1; 2 Cor. 1:1; Gal. 1:1; etc.) is not motivated by any egoism. Rather, Paul is simply asserting the authority that God bestowed on him so that all might recognize this authority and benefit from it. In particular, Paul wants the readers of his epistle to Timothy to acknowledge his apostolic authority so that they may in turn respect Timothy, to whom Paul, the teacher of the Gentiles, has given certain instructions. It is for Timothy's sake that Paul here puts forth his exalted apostolic status.

༄ ༄ ༄ ༄ ༄

8   Therefore I intend the men to pray in every place, lifting up holy hands, without wrath and questioning.

Therefore, because the Church should pray, Paul **intends** that **the men** of every one of the city's eucharistic assemblies should **pray**. (This is not simply Paul's preference, but his will and directive. The word used is the Gr. *boulomai*, cognate with *boulema* or "will"; compare its use in Rom. 9:19.) The men **in every place** refers to the men offering the public prayers at the services, which were held in small groups and house-churches throughout the city. In every place or cell group in which the believers assemble for worship, the men are to take the liturgical lead. This does not mean that women are to remain utterly mute. We know from Paul's instructions in 1 Corinthians 11:4 that they may prophesy. But taking the lead in audible public prayer (or liturgical prayer in the Sunday services) remains the task of the men.

The men must offer these public liturgical prayers **lifting up holy hands**. Lifting up the hands from a standing position was the normal posture for prayer. St. Paul's exhortation and main concern is that these be *holy* hands, undefiled by sins of **wrath and questioning** or disputing. The Lord said that whenever one stands to pray, one must forgive (Mark 11:25), for effective prayer cannot arise from an unforgiving and resentful heart. Likewise, St. Paul here tells Timothy that the leaders of his church must pray in peace, having laid aside all angry arguments. They cannot quarrel and debate over their evening agape meal and then a moment later stand to offer prayer acceptable to God. They must take their meals and fellowship in peace and love if God is to hear their prayers.

ॐ ॐ ॐ ॐ ॐ

9 Likewise, women should adorn themselves with respectable deportment, with modesty and restraint, not with braids and gold or pearls or costly apparel;

10 but as is proper for women professing godly-piety, through good works.

11 Let a woman learn in quietness, in all sub-mission.

12 I do not allow a woman to teach or have author-ity over a man, but to be in quietness.

13 For it was Adam who was first formed, then Eve.

14 And Adam was not deceived, but the woman, being completely deceived, came to be in trans-gression.

15 But she will be saved through the childbearing if they remain in faith and love and holiness with restraint.

Having given direction to the men in v. 8, St. Paul then turns to give similar directions to the **women** in vv. 9–15. They must do **likewise** as their men; as the men were to avoid temptations to quar-rel, so the women too must avoid the temptation to put themselves forward. It seems that the women in Ephesus were overstepping the prescribed bounds. As wealthy women, they were perhaps used to getting their own way and took the opportunity to promote them-selves as teachers with authority in the Church. St. Paul directs them to a self-effacing humility. The men of Ephesus liked to quarrel, and it seems that the women joined in the fray. Paul directs them to join their men in being quiet, peaceable, and harmonious.

In directing the women into this harmony and humility, Paul deals first of all with their external temptations to ostentation. Rich women of that day spent an inordinate amount of time in self-beautification, using elaborate false **braids** fastened with costly pins and combs; they spent great sums on **gold or pearls**; they draped themselves with **costly apparel**. Though these are not wrong in themselves, Paul cites them as elements of these women's obsession with outward appearance, and it is this obsession with wealthy self-display that is rebuked rather than the externals themselves. **Women professing godly-piety** do not need such ornate externals, and their consuming concern with them gives the lie to their piety. If they would **adorn themselves** fittingly, let them do it with **respectable deportment**, carrying themselves and dressing with **modesty and restraint**. As is **proper** for women claiming to be devout, let their true beauty and adornment be in their **good works** of mercy to the poor. In their wealth, these women have a tendency to strut, to strive to impress others through their riches. St. Paul encourages them to value rather the humility that delights in helping others, not the pride that competes with them.

After dealing with the temptation to ostentation, the apostle proceeds to deal with the inner temptation to power. These women seem to have been using their social position to promote themselves as teachers in the Church. This is unacceptable for St. Paul; he directs that the women **learn in quietness, in all submission**, not teach in all authority, in loud enthusiasm. Indeed, he categorically forbids women to exercise such a role, saying he does **not allow a woman to teach or have authority over a man**. Rather, she must **be in quietness**.

Because this apostolic teaching has recently generated a great deal of controversy, we should examine it in greater detail. In particular, we should determine exactly what St. Paul is forbidding. He is not forbidding to women any and all speech in church, for in Corinth (a big city every bit as pagan as Ephesus) he allowed women to pray (presumably quietly, as members of the congregation) and to prophesy (aloud, as prophets speaking to the assembly), provided they were decently veiled (1 Cor. 11:5). Paul does not enjoin absolute silence, but "quietness" or stillness (Gr. *hesuchia*, from which we get the word "hesychast," one who practices inner stillness).

The women in Ephesus tended to stand up in the agape meals/eucharistic assemblies and offer authoritative teaching as the presbyters/elders did—perhaps because some were married to presbyters/elders. It is precisely this presbyteral authority that St. Paul denies them. The presbyters are the shepherds and teachers (Eph. 4:11) who thereby have to teach the Church with authority, rightly defining the word of truth. The presbyters are the ones who are to rule the Church and watch over the souls of the people (Heb. 13:17). Paul does not permit the women to do this work. Their role is rather to learn, not to teach; they are to remain "in quietness" and inner stillness, "in all submission," following the leadership of their husbands and the teachers of the Church. (This directive, of course, does not ban women from all teaching whatsoever. Priscilla, after all, taught Apollos; see Acts 18:26. Paul here refers to the authoritative teaching of the pastoral office.)

We may add in passing that such submission (Gr. *upotage*) is not inherently degrading, nor does such humility detract from one's essential dignity. For just as the wives were to submit to their husbands (Gr. *upotasso*, Eph. 5:24), so Christ will finally submit to the Father (Gr. *upotasso*, 1 Cor. 15:28), and yet Christ remains equal to the Father as one of the Holy Trinity. Christ's submission to the Father does not mean that He is of less value or is hypostatically inferior to the Father. Likewise, the submission St. Paul here demands from the women does not mean they are of less value than their husbands or the leaders of the Church. Submission and leadership involve function and task and do not indicate essential inner value.

What is the rationale for St. Paul's directives? The apostle does not base his restriction of women from the pastoral office on any contemporary conditions. He does not say that they may not be ordained because they did not at that time have sufficient education, nor that such authority would not have been acceptable to society at large. Rather, he bases his restriction on the nature of the gender roles as created by God at the beginning. In the beginning, even before the Fall had introduced sin into the world, **it was Adam who was first formed, then Eve** (see the creation story in Gen. 2), and as the first-formed, it was Adam who was given authority over his wife. Note that in the creation story, Adam names the animals as master over them (Gen. 2:20), and then names his wife as well, expressing his leadership role within their marriage (Gen. 2:23). Paul says that Adam had authority over Eve based on the priority of his creation, and this authority remains as the paradigm and model in Christian marriage.

To this Paul adds another reason, also based on the primordial gender roles. At the Fall, **Adam was not deceived** (Gr. *apatao*); he sinned deliberately and knowingly, with his eyes wide open. He willfully turned away from his God—which is why we die "in Adam," not "in Eve" (1 Cor. 15:22). It was otherwise with Eve. When she left her position of submission to Adam and assumed a leadership role, she was **completely deceived** (Gr. *exapatao*—a more intensive verb) and thus **came to be in transgression**. When she assumed an authority and leadership role not belonging to her, disaster ensued, and for St. Paul this remains as a warning of what happens when women usurp a leadership that is not theirs.

This does not mean, however, that women are under some special curse. Far from it. The woman also **will be saved** by the grace of Christ, even as her husband will. But she must remain in her proper sphere—that of **the childbearing** role, tending her family and finding her salvation within this context. That is, women must **remain in faith and love and holiness**, serving as the disciples of Jesus, walking **with restraint** and modesty. They must not agitate to seize a role in the Church not given by God, but walk before Him in peace.

We may also add that today this domestic context is considerably enlarged and may include gainful employment outside the walls of home. Whatever the pluses or minuses of women being in the workplace, it remains true that Paul does not here forbid such a possibility. (See the example of the businesswoman Lydia, Acts

16:14.) The apostle simply says that Christian wives are to work out their salvation in a domestic setting, following their husbands' lead, not in a position of leadership in the Church, ruling over their husbands. Further, situations such as infertile or childless couples are not here his concern.

❧ EXCURSUS:
ON PAUL'S BAN ON WOMEN CLERGY IN CHURCH HISTORY

St. Paul's teaching forbidding women to hold pastoral office is clear enough to the unbiased reader. Some today suggest, however, that Paul was only giving counsel for the situation in Ephesus in the first century, and that we should not make his teaching the universal norm for the Church throughout the centuries. How did the Church apply Paul's teaching regarding women and the pastoral office? Did the Fathers regard it as merely situational? Put differently, is St. Paul's teaching, given here, part of Holy Tradition? To answer this question, we will look at how the Fathers viewed women's eligibility for the pastoral office in the centuries following St. Paul.

In the *Didache* (or *Teaching of the Twelve Apostles*), dated about AD 100, the author speaks of bishops and deacons thus: "Appoint for yourselves bishops and deacons worthy of the Lord, men who are meek and not lovers of money, true and approved" (ch. 15). The word here rendered "men" is the Greek *aner*, used only of men and not women. Had women been allowed to occupy these offices, doubtless the author would have used the more general word *anthropos*, "human being."

Tertullian, writing from North Africa in the late second and early third century, said, "It is not permitted to a woman to speak in the church, but neither is it permitted her to teach, nor to baptize, nor to offer [the Eucharist], nor to claim to herself a lot in any masculine function, not to say in any priestly office" (*On the Veiling of Virgins*, ch. 9).

Origen, writing in the early third century, has this to say: "It is not permitted that women teach or exercise authority over men. [Paul] desires that the women teach good by training young women to purity, not young men, for it is improper that a woman be the teacher of a man" (*Homilies on Is. 6:3*).

St. Epiphanius of Cyprus, writing in the late fourth century, says, "When we come to the New Testament, if the priesthood is said to be a commission for women . . . to no one else than Mary should the office of priest be committed. But, from her so great an honor was withheld, though from her womb and her bosom she took the King of all" (*Panarion*, ch. 79).

St. John Chrysostom, who died in AD 407, said this: "[Paul's word] 'I permit no woman to teach' . . . concerns teachings given from the tribunal, speeches made in public, which is a priestly function. But he does not particularly forbid exhorting or counseling [her husband]" (*Homily 1 on Priscilla and Aquila*, ch. 3). He also said in another book, "The things I have just mentioned [works of asceticism] can be performed by many of the faithful, not only men, but also women. But when it is a question of the government of the church and of direction of so many souls, let the whole female sex withdraw from such a task—and likewise the majority of men!" (*On the Priesthood*, ch. 2).

Chrysostom's contemporary, Theodore of Mopsuestia (who died in 428), writes, "It is plain that the text, 'I do not permit women to teach' refers to public situations; women must not teach in the assembly, for Paul certainly did not forbid women . . . to educate their unbelieving husbands" (*Commentary on 1 Timothy 2*).

From these citations, we can discern the mind of the Church. In this present passage, Paul was not simply speaking of a local and temporary situation. He was expressing an abiding apostolic principle, and the Church in the succeeding centuries understood this to be so.

§VI.   Bishops' and Deacons' Qualifications (3:1–13)

ॐ ॐ ॐ ॐ ॐ

3 1 Faithful *is* the word: If anyone aspires to *the* episcopate, he desires a good work.

2 It is necessary, therefore, for the bishop to be irreproachable, the husband of one wife, sober, restrained, respectable, hospitable, *able to teach,*

3 not *given to* wine, not a striker, but forbearing, not quarrelsome, not a lover of money.

4 He must be one who presides over his own house well, having his children in submission with all reverence

5 (for if anyone does not know how to preside over *his* own house, how will he care for the church of God?),

6 not a neophyte, lest he become conceited and fall into the devil's judgment.

7 And it is also necessary to have a good witness from the ones outside, lest he fall into reproach and the snare of the devil.

Many in Ephesus desire to be teachers (1:7), and Paul instructs Timothy to ordain to such an office only those suited to the task. Paul quotes the proverbial wisdom and **faithful word** of the Church: **If anyone aspires to *the* episcopate, he desires a good work.** Therefore, Timothy must ensure that only good men undertake this work.

The words "episcopate" and "bishop" require some explanation, for the terms have changed somewhat over the years. In the first century, the terms "bishop" (Gr. *episcopos*) and "elder" (Gr. *presbuteros*) were used interchangeably, indicating one and the same office. Thus Luke reports Paul as addressing these Ephesian "elders" in Acts 20:17 and telling them that God had made them "bishops" (Acts

20:28). Each city, with its several house churches or gatherings, had its plurality of these bishop/elders, and these clergy all looked to one of their number as their head, though this man had no special title. We see the pattern most clearly in Jerusalem, where there were a number of elders (see Acts 15:4) having James as their head (cf. Acts 12:17; 15:13; Gal. 2:12). With the growth in importance of this head by the early second century, the terminology underwent a change. From the time of Ignatius of Antioch (who died about 107), the term "presbyter" or "elder" was used to describe each of the pastors, with the term "bishop" reserved for the head pastor alone. Henceforth he was known as *the* bishop, assisted by his fellow elders.

But at the time of Paul's writing to Timothy, this change in terminology and the growth of the office of head pastor of the city lay still in the future. When Paul here describes the bishop, he describes the pastor *per se*, whether the head pastor (later called the bishop) or any of his pastoral colleagues (later called elders). The bishops whose qualifications Paul here sets forth were the pastors called to rule over the various house churches of Ephesus.

Paul's main concern is for the character of the bishops. **The bishop** (or pastor) must be **irreproachable** (Gr. *anepilemptos*), of such well-known integrity that to accuse him of unworthy conduct would be unthinkable. He must be **the husband of one wife**. That is, he must not have been divorced and now married to a second (or third!) wife. Paul's insistence on the bishop having but one wife cannot mean simply that he must not be a polygamist. There is no suggestion in any of Paul's epistles that polygamy was an option in the Church, and in the epistles detailing relations between husband and wife, such as Ephesians, Colossians, and 1 Corinthians, such a possibility is not considered—doubtless because of the rarity of its occurrence. Also, Paul's insistence on the bishop having but one wife does not mean that the bishop *must* be married and may not be a celibate, since celibacy is exactly what Paul proffers as the ideal (see 1 Cor. 7:1, 7). We may think that Paul would certainly have allowed celibate church leaders, since he was one himself. Paul's concern here is for the bishop's stability of life, as evidenced by the absence of divorce.

The bishop or pastor must also be **sober** (Gr. *nephalios*), meaning not simply that he shuns alcoholic intoxication, but also that he maintains an inner vigilance and spiritual balance. He is not subject to manic-depressive imbalances, soaring to the heights and then plummeting to the depths. The bishop must be able to stay on an even keel.

Further, Paul says the potential pastor must be **restrained** (Gr. *sophron*), a quality commended in women as well (compare the cognate in 2:9, 15). That is, the pastor must be modest and self-controlled, able to command respect by his gracious and dignified bearing. This resembles the quality of being **respectable** (Gr. *kosmios*)—which quality is commended in women also (see 2:9). The word *kosmios* denotes not simply outward respectability (with all its modern connotations of dullness and blandness). Rather, one who is *kosmios* has an honesty and propriety that publicly commend his inner goodness.

The man Paul commends to Timothy for ordination is **hospitable** (Gr. *philoxenos*—lit., "stranger-loving")—one who delights to welcome the many strangers from other Christian communities who inevitably pass through Ephesus. Such a man must be *able to* **teach** (Gr. *didaktikos*), meaning that he must have not only the necessary learning, but also a teacher's heart—he must be one who delights to teach and by his enthusiasm makes the teaching credible.

Moreover, the man must be **not *given to* wine** (Gr. *paroinos*), with a tendency to get drunk. He must not be **a striker** (Gr. *plektes*, cognate with the classical *plektizomai*, a verb used for the beating of one's breast). A *striker* easily cuffs the ears of his subordinates (a common thing in antiquity) and irritably lashes out when crossed, like a bully. The potential leader must be the opposite—one who is **forbearing**, gentle and yielding (Gr. *epeikes*), **not quarrelsome** (Gr. *amaxos*), one who instinctively avoids a fight.

Also, he must be **not a lover of money** (Gr. *aphilarguros*) or one who has a weakness for bribes. He must value spiritual riches and the commendation of God, so that his conscience cannot be bought or swayed by the rich. Further, he must be **one who presides over his own house well, having his children in submission with**

all reverence. The word translated "preside" (Gr. *proistami*, lit. "to stand before") means to rule, to manage. The pastor's family must be respectful of authority and not out of control, for this would indicate a defect in the pastor himself. If his use of authority is such that it alienates *his* **own house**, then obviously he cannot **care** and attentively watch over **the church of God** either. A pastor is first and foremost a father, and one may discern what kind of a father a man is by observing his own family.

Also, the potential leader must not be **a neophyte** (Gr. *neophutos*, lit., "newly-planted") or a recent convert. Authority given too early, when suffering has not aged and matured the spirit, can too easily cause one to **become conceited** and blinded with arrogance of office. By abusing his authority, such a one would **fall into the devil's judgment**, incurring the same condemnation the devil did when pride filled his heart and he fell from grace.

Finally, the pastor must also **have a good witness from the ones outside**, a spotless reputation. Otherwise, he may **fall into reproach and the snare** set by **the devil**. If people know the candidate to be a man of vices, they will reproach him for it, causing him to harden his heart as he perseveres in his sins, with the result that he falls headlong into Satan's trap as he sears his conscience and ruins his salvation.

Paul outlines these qualifications as the ones Timothy must strive to discern in any whom he would ordain. The pastor must be worthy (Gr. *axios*) of such an office by his possession of these qualities. Timothy is not to look for some hidden and subjective "calling" to the office in potential candidates. Such an inner sense of vocation may be assumed. Paul gives him the task to confirm the candidate's aspirations and sense of call by discerning these moral qualities in his life. If the candidate lacks these qualities, his own conviction of vocation counts for nothing.

꒰ꑸ꒱ ꒰ꑸ꒱ ꒰ꑸ꒱ ꒰ꑸ꒱ ꒰ꑸ꒱

8   Deacons likewise must be reverent, not double-tongued, not indulging in much wine, not *given to* shameful gain,

---

> 9 having the mystery of the Faith in a clean conscience.
>
> 10 And also let these first be proven, then let them serve, being blameless.
>
> 11 Women likewise must be reverent, not slanderers, *but* sober, faithful in all things.
>
> 12 Let deacons be husbands of one wife, presiding well over *their* children and *their* own houses.
>
> 13 For those who have served well acquire a good rank for themselves and much boldness in the Faith in Christ Jesus.

The other officeholder that Paul commended to Timothy's supervision was the deacon. (One may see the two local offices working together in Phil. 1:1.) The diaconate institutionalizes the Church's servanthood, for the title "deacon" (Gr. *diakonos*) means "servant" and is cognate with the verb "to serve" (Gr. *diakoneo*) in vv. 10, 13. The deacons performed the physical aspects of the Church's servanthood, such as the collection and dispersal of alms and the visiting of the sick.

Such a public and important office must **likewise** be filled only by men of integrity, like the episcopate or office of pastor. That is, like the bishops, the **deacons** also must be **reverent** (Gr. *semnos*), dignified, and noble; they must not **indulge** in **much wine** nor be *given to* shameful gain, willing to take a bribe to favor one over another as he distributes the Church's alms (see v. 3). Deacons must not be **double-tongued** (Gr. *dilogos*, lit. "two-word"), telling each person what he wants to hear as a dishonest flatterer. Because they have the special task of handling the Church's money, deacons must have and hold **the mystery of the Faith in a clean conscience**. The Faith, revealed as a *mystery* (Gr. *musterion*) to the initiated, the Christians, must not be defiled by the deacons holding to it with a dishonest life.

In order to ensure this, the deacons must **first be proven** and tested. The Church must observe carefully how faithfully and honestly they fulfill the nondiaconal tasks given to them since their baptism. If they fulfill them well and are **blameless** in their lives, **then** and only then they may be ordained and may **serve** as deacons (Gr. *diakoneo*).

As with the bishops, the quality of the deacons' lives may be gauged as one observes their families. Their **women** or wives must be **reverent** (Gr. *semnos*) like their husbands (compare v. 8). They must not be **slanderers** or malicious gossips (Gr. *diabolos*, lit. "devils"). Rather they must be **sober** and balanced in spirit (Gr. *nephalios*, see v. 2), **faithful in all things**, diligently performing the tasks undertaken. Deacons, like the bishops, must be the **husbands of one wife** and not divorced and remarried. They too must **preside well over** *their* **children and** *their* **own houses**, showing they have the stability to keep them under control by their love.

One might be tempted to despise the diaconate, thinking it lower than the rank of bishop or overseeing pastor, and therefore to think it does not much matter what sort of men undertake this work. On the contrary, says St. Paul, **those who have served well** as deacons (Gr. *diakoneo*) **acquire a good rank for themselves**. The word here translated "rank" is the Greek *bathmos*, meaning "grade or step." Paul's meaning seems to be that those who have served well as deacons have attained to a rank that is good in itself, one that gives them the right to have **much boldness in the Faith in Christ Jesus**. In their service in the Church of God, they may approach God with boldness, knowing they have served Him well.

A note may be added regarding the "women" (Gr. *gunaikas*) mentioned in v. 11, since some commentators have taken these to be woman deacons or deaconesses. This supposition is quite anachronistic. Mention of women deacons does not appear in post-New Testament literature until the third-century church order the *Didascalia*, and it would seem clear that the order of women deacons does not actually arise in the Church until that time. The women mentioned by Paul in this section therefore are not women deacons, but the wives of the deacons themselves. If they were women deacons, not only would their complete disappearance from written history be hard to explain, but the coherence and order of this part of the epistle would be compromised also. For this would mean that Paul mentioned male deacons in vv. 8–10, women deacons in v. 11, and then male deacons again in v. 12. If there *were* women deacons, one would have expected Paul to deal with the men first and then the women, and not to insert his instructions for one in the midst of his instructions for the other. It makes more sense to read the entire passage as describing male deacons only, mentioning the women only insofar as their qualities reflect on their husbands (just as the households of bishops reflect on them, vv. 4–5). It is significant too that deacons are expected to be the husband of one wife, and there is no mention of the women deacons being also the wives of one husband! In short, it may or may not be expedient for the Church to establish an order of deaconesses today, but it must be acknowledged that the present passage says nothing about it.

§VII.   Timothy and Conduct in the Church (3:14–16)

> ॐ ॐ ॐ ॐ ॐ
>
> 14 These things I am writing to you, hoping to come to you soon;
> 15 but if I am delayed, you may know how one ought to conduct oneself in God's house, which is *the* church of the living God, *the* pillar and firm *buttress* of the Truth.
> 16 And confessedly great is the mystery of piety:
> He who was manifested in *the* flesh,
> was justified in *the* Spirit,
> seen by angels,
> heralded among *the* nations,
> believed *on* in *the* world,
> taken up in glory.

Paul then explains the reason for all these instructions. He is **hoping to come** to Ephesus **soon** and will then give a fuller explanation. But he is **writing these things** now just in case he is **delayed**. It is essential for Timothy to **know how one ought to conduct oneself**

in God's house—that is, in *the* **church of the living God**. These high standards are incumbent on the men and women (2:8–15) and on the bishops and deacons (3:1–13) because of the Church's great holiness. The Church is no mere philosophical school, but rather God's house itself, the place where the Lord of Hosts manifests Himself. When Israel assembled in the wilderness as a solemn gathering (in Hebrew, *qahal*, in Greek, *ecclesia*, in English, "church"; see Acts 7:38), then God dwelt among them in power. In the same way, when the Christians gather together, they too are God's church, the dwelling-place of the living God of all the earth, before whom all the pagan gods are but phantoms and idols. "Who among us shall dwell with the devouring fire?" asked the prophet Isaiah (Is. 33:14). God is a Fire consuming wickedness and sin, and yet He dwells in the midst of the Christians, manifesting Himself to them in their assemblies, their church. The Christians must know how to live in holiness if they would call the Holy One into their midst.

As God's dwelling-place, the Church is *the* **pillar and firm buttress** of the eternal **Truth** of the Gospel. As a "pillar" (Gr. *stulos*), it upholds and displays the Truth, holding it aloft for all the world to see. As the "firm buttress" (Gr. *edraioma*, cognate with *edraios*, "firm"), it keeps the Truth from being overthrown, allowing it to stand for all ages. Given the cosmic and eternal importance of their gatherings, the Christians must live in accordance with it, supporting the truth with the holiness of their lives.

They can recognize the greatness of the Church (and the necessity for holiness in her) from the popular hymn that expresses how **great is the mystery of piety**, the Christian Faith. This "piety" and way of pleasing God were not manifested before, but now, as a true "mystery," God has revealed it to the initiates, the Christian faithful. (The word "mystery," Gr. *musterion,* refers to a reality hidden from the masses, but revealed to the select few initiates—in this case, the Christians.) And all acknowledge the greatness of this faith, for it is **confessedly** great—that is, its greatness is the subject of common confession. For all confess the greatness of the Church and of her Faith when they confess the greatness of Jesus in their hymn.

The hymn (composed some years earlier, perhaps, and sung at

the Eucharist?) is short and powerful, consisting of three pairs of contrasts, each one describing the majesty of Jesus. (The parallelisms are more apparent in the Greek.)

First the hymn says He was **manifested in *the* flesh, was justified in *the* Spirit** (Gr. *ephanerothe en sarki, edikaiothe en pneumati*). That is, though Jesus was "manifested" and incarnate in lowly weakness "in the flesh," He was later "justified" and vindicated "in the Spirit" by His Resurrection from the dead in power. Further, He was **seen by angels, heralded among *the* nations** (Gr. *ophthe aggelois, ekeruxthe en ethnesin*). That is, He was first secretly "seen" and beheld only "by angels" (for example, at His Resurrection; see Luke 24:4–7), but then later "heralded" and preached "in the nations" and on the open world stage. Finally, the hymn describes Him as **believed *on* in *the* world, taken up in glory** (Gr. *episteuthe en kosmo, anelemphthe en doxe*). That is, Jesus was acknowledged here in the world below and glorified in the world above. Both heaven and earth celebrate His glory.

In all these three pairs, the greatness of Jesus is expressed, and each contrasting pair shows how that greatness increases: first Christ is lowly, then He is exalted. He was born in the flesh in lowliness, then vindicated in the Spirit at His Resurrection; He was at first seen only by angels, then proclaimed among all the Gentiles; He was at first acknowledged on earth, then by all in heaven in His ascended glory. The hymn the Christians sing at their services reveals the true greatness of the Church, for the Church proclaims and manifests such a mighty Savior. Those who proclaim this great Faith must live lives worthy of it.

§VIII. Teachings of Demons (4:1–5)

ॐ ॐ ॐ ॐ ॐ

4 1 But the Spirit expressly says that in later times some will leave the Faith, paying attention to deceptive spirits and teachings of demons
  2 through the hypocrisy of lying words, *spoken by those* seared in *their* own conscience,

> 3 *those who* forbid marrying and *enjoin* abstaining from foods which God created for partaking with thanksgiving by those who have faith and who really-know the Truth.
>
> 4 For every creation of God *is* good and nothing *is to be* cast-aside if it is received with thanksgiving,
>
> 5 for it is sanctified through *the* Word of God and petition.

The apostle continues with his instructions about how one should conduct oneself in the Church, giving a warning against the growing heresy of gnosticism (from the Gr. *gnosis*, or "knowledge"). Gnosticism was a movement, a syncretistic tendency, rather than a rival church or religion. The teachers of the various gnostic philosophies passed themselves off as offering a higher, more spiritual form of Christianity. Paul's version of the Christian Faith might be adequate for the dull and immature, they said, but *their* version was for the elite! The heresy had already found fertile soil in the Lycus Valley in Asia Minor, and Paul had already warned the Colossians about it in his epistle to them. Now, as the heresy continues to spread, he warns Timothy of it as well.

One should not be surprised at such counterfeits, he says. For in the prophecies of the Church, **the Spirit expressly says that in later times some will leave the Faith**. Paul was used to such prophecies, for in many communities there lived prophets who received messages from God and stood up to declare them. Some prophets spoke and confirmed Paul's own apostolic mission (Acts 13:2); the prophet Agabus stood up and predicted his arrest (Acts 21:11); and Timothy himself had heard the prophets speak about his own ministry when he was first ordained (4:14). Though we do not know when and where the prophets predicted this future rise of counterfeit faith, their warnings gave the Church time to prepare for it and resist it. Forewarned is forearmed!

For the spreading heresy, St. Paul warns, is quite beguiling. Whatever its promoters might say, however, it constitutes not another variety of Christian Faith, but apostasy from it, and those who **pay attention** to its teaching are in fact listening to **deceptive spirits and teachings of demons**. The promoters themselves are not men of holiness either. They speak **hypocrisy** (Gr. *upokrisis*) and **lying words** (Gr. *pseudologos*), for they promise freedom from sin while they are all the time enslaved to it. In fact, their refusal to heed any warning has burned their **own conscience**, so that it is **seared** as with a branding iron (Gr. *kausteriazo*) and is totally numb, insensitive to the voice of God and unable to warn of the dangers of sin. This allows them to sin freely with no twinges of alarm. Obviously they cannot be guides to holiness as they claim!

As examples of their teachings, Paul quotes two of their prohibitions: they **forbid marrying** and *enjoin* **abstaining** from certain **foods**, probably meat. Enjoying marriage and eating such food, they say, are only for the carnal who do not have true knowledge of God. The truly spiritual abstain from sex and from meat-eating, for these are barriers to God. This gnostic teaching had nothing to do with the Church's delight in celibacy and fasting. At certain periods Paul himself enjoined abstinence from sex for the purpose of prayer (see 1 Cor. 7:5), and the Lord assumed that His disciples would fast (Matt. 6:16). The Church takes for granted that marriage and all foods (including meat) are good, but that one may forgo them for the sake of discipline and the attainment of an even higher good. The gnostics were different, for they insisted that sex, meat-eating, and wine-drinking were bad in themselves.

Paul denounces this error. The food the gnostic teachers reject as evil and as a barrier to knowing God was **created** by **God** Himself so that we could **partake with thanksgiving**. God made this food to be eaten with gratitude, not rejected as evil. He created it to feed **those who have faith and who really-know** and recognize **the Truth**. (Obviously, then, the gnostics do not know the Truth as they claim!) Indeed, **every creation of God**—including the foods rejected and **cast-aside** by the gnostic teachers—is **good**, and the gnostics fail to understand the nature of creation or the goodness of the Creator. If God created these things, by definition they must therefore be good, for the good God would not create something bad in itself. All things must be **received** and used for their proper purpose, provided they are received **with thanksgiving**. Such things are not barriers to holiness, for the Ephesian Christians themselves have been **sanctified** and made holy by God (Gr. *agiazo*, cognate with *agios*, "holy"). How and when were they thus made holy? They were sanctified **through *the* Word of God and petition**.

This "Word of God" (Gr. *logos theou*) is the original creative Word spoken by God at creation. For He said, "Let there be light," and light was created (Gen. 1:3); all that is exists only because God spoke it into existence by His sovereign word of power. The primordial and creative Word of the holy God suffices to charge creation with a natural holiness and acceptability to Him. Also, the created realities of marriage and food are sanctified by our prayerful "petition" (Gr. *enteuxis*). When we give thanks to God, blessing Him over our food before we eat it, we thereby offer Him a petition to accept our eating and to bless our food. Thanksgiving for the good things of creation thus also renders them holy before their Creator, and we may partake of them in peace. The promoters of gnosticism troubled the simple-hearted faithful and told them that these pleasures were suspect. Paul knows the gnostics teach not the truth of God, but the teachings of demons, who would destroy God's creation. He tells Timothy to beware of such heresy and to tell his people to beware it also.

Paul's affirmation of the goodness of creation reveals the Christian Faith to be a world-affirming faith and a religion of joy. The world misunderstands our asceticism, thinking it to be a hatred of pleasure, and they slander the Christians, labeling them ill-tempered and dour fanatics. These verses reveal how wrong the world is in its understanding of the Church and her asceticism. Orthodoxy confesses that though creation is fallen and in need of redemption, it remains fundamentally very good (see Gen. 1:31), and it delights in God's handiwork. Food is good, marriage is good, life is good. We are not only to love our Creator; we are to love what He has made. Christian ecology, Orthodox concern for the environment, is rooted in this appreciation of the works of God.

§IX.   Timothy to Persevere as an Example (4:6–16)

ৡ৾ ৡ৾ ৡ৾ ৡ৾ ৡ৾

6   In putting these things before the brothers, you will be a good servant of Christ Jesus, nourished on the words of the Faith and of the good teaching which you have followed along.

7   But reject profane and old-wives' myths. Train yourself for piety,

8   for bodily training is of little profit, but piety is profitable for all things, having promise for the present life and for the *life* to come.

9   Faithful *is* the word, and worthy of all acceptance.

10 For to this *end* we toil and *strive in* contest, because we have hoped on a living God, who is *the* Savior of all men, especially of *the* faithful.

11 Order and teach these things.

Timothy might be reluctant to enter into the fray in this matter, but he must do so anyway. For **in putting these things before the brothers** he will be **a good servant of Christ Jesus**. That is, he is to offer the teaching he has found to be profitable himself—the **words of the Faith** on which he himself has been **nourished** and brought up. All his life he **followed along** this **good teaching**, and now he must humbly share this with his brothers. The word translated "followed along" is the Greek *parakoloutheo*. It means "to follow with the mind," and thus also to investigate, which is its meaning in Luke 1:3. Paul uses this word to stress the practical nature of what Timothy is to teach. He must not spend his time passing on **profane and old wives' myths**, like the would-be Jewish teachers (see 1:4, 7). Rather, he must pass on the practical piety he has investigated and found to be reliable and life-giving. He has discovered that it works for him, and it will work for others too.

Unlike those who specialize in myths, Timothy's teaching results in **piety** (Gr. *eusebia*), an increase of love from a pure heart (1:5), not just mental exercise. Paul instructs Timothy to **train** himself for this. The word translated "train" is the Greek *gumnazo*, cognate with the word "training" (Gr. *gumnasia*) in v. 8. The word has an athletic feel to it, related to the gymnasium found in every Greek town, where the young male athletes (Gr. *gumnos*) would train naked. Just as pagan boys spend hours in the gymnasium, spending energy on **bodily training**, so Timothy must spend that time on spiritual training for piety. The Jewish myths are fit for old wives; *he* is to engage in the true manly pursuit of godliness. This is a better use of his time than the physical workout on which other young men spend their time, for their training is **of little profit**, but Timothy's training for **piety is profitable for all things**, holding out **promise for the present life** in this age and also **for the *life* to come**. To spend one's hours in the gymnasium produces muscles that will one day atrophy and fade, but to spend that time instead in pursuit of God in prayer and Scripture reading will result in spiritual power that the years cannot touch. Everyone knows this: **faithful** is that **word** and proverb, **worthy of all acceptance**.

It is **to this *end*** that Paul and his colleagues **toil and *strive in* contest**—to obtain joy in this life and in the next. The word rendered here "strive in contest" is the Greek *agonizo*, cognate with *agon*, or "race" (so rendered in Heb. 12:1), an image of straining in an athletic contest to win the victory. St. Paul uses this image to describe his apostolic ministry—laboring and running the race to win the prize. He **hopes** in God, fixing all his hopes on Him, like an athlete competing in the games—to win the reward from Him.

Paul knows that he serves **a living God**, not a dead and powerless one like the pagan idols, and as a living God, He is able to reward those who serve Him. He is the **Savior of all men**, for He is the One and only God of all the earth. God calls all men everywhere, even the pagans at the farthest end of the earth, to believe in Him, for His Son died to ransom them all. (Thus the **faithful**, the Christians, who accept Him are **especially** His people, for in them His ransom bears fruit.) Knowing that God is the Savior of all, Paul toils and strives to bring the Gospel to all. As Paul strives for the salvation of all, so Timothy also must **order and teach these things**, striving to bring all to salvation as well, assuring them that their efforts at piety will bring an eternal reward.

> ෴ ෴ ෴ ෴ ෴
>
> 12 Let no one despise your youth, but become a pattern for the faithful in word, conduct, love, faith, and purity.
> 13 Until I come, pay attention to reading, to exhortation and teaching.
> 14 Do not neglect the *spiritual* gift in you which was given to you through prophecy with laying on of hands of the *council of* elders.
> 15 Study these things, be in them, that your progress may be manifest to all.
> 16 Fix *your attention* on yourself and the teaching, remain in them, for *in* doing this you will save both yourself and those hearing you.

Some in Ephesus might **despise** Timothy's **youth** and look down on him. Timothy was about twenty-nine years of age at this time (assuming him to have been seventeen years old when he first joined Paul)—far too young (some thought) for him to order and teach the older would-be teachers of Ephesus. Why, they might ask, should they consent to be taught and corrected by one younger than themselves? But Timothy should not be intimidated by them. Yet neither should he assert his authority in a confrontational style. Rather, he must **become a pattern** and example (Gr. *tupos*, "type") **for the faithful**. He must inspire them to follow him and let the moral authority of his life speak for him. In his **word** and speech, in all his **conduct**, he must prove himself their true leader, commending his authority by both his word and his deed. In particular, he must excel in **love** for the brothers, in **faith** or faithfulness to God, in sexual **purity** before the world. (Paul especially stresses this last, *purity*, perhaps because of the temptations characteristic of youth; see 5:2.)

Until Paul arrives in Ephesus, Timothy is to **pay attention** and devote himself to a ministry of education (1:3). That is, he must concentrate on public **reading** of the Scriptures to the Church—a necessity in those days, when most people did not possess their own copies of the Scriptures. Timothy must also concentrate on **exhortation** (Gr. *paraklesis*), encouraging them to holiness in imitation of what was read. Further, after reading, he must give **teaching** (Gr. *didaskalia*), showing them how the Scriptures (meaning here the Old Testament) are fulfilled in Christ and the Church.

In this task, he does not have to rely on his natural abilities alone. A *spiritual* **gift** (Gr. *charisma*) of teaching has been **given** to him by God, accompanied by a **prophecy** when the *council of* **elders** or presbyters ordained him with the **laying on of hands**. With the charismatic gift of teaching (see Eph. 4:11) given in such glorious circumstances, with all the presbyters praying and the prophets speaking, how can he **neglect** such an endowment and fail in his task? How can he quail before men who despise his youthfulness and be silent, allowing them to teach error? Surely he can find the courage to speak up and teach with authority, as the *prophecy* commissioned him to do at his ordination.

This work must be Timothy's constant occupation; he must **study these things**. The word translated "study" is the Greek *meletao*, meaning "to cultivate, take pains with, practice, meditate." The education of the faithful for their growth in holiness must be Timothy's all-consuming passion; he must **be in them** (the virtues mentioned in v. 12) and be immersed in such work. In this way, his spiritual **progress** will be **manifest to all**. Then all those in Ephesus will see his worth, despite his youth. If Timothy will **fix** his attention on himself and the teaching and give himself over to it, then he will **save** not only himself. His spiritual maturity will give credibility to his teaching so that others will more easily accept it, and he will thus save **those hearing** him also. This is his task until Paul arrives.

Paul's counsel to Timothy can be fruitfully applied to clergy today, of whatever age. A parish priest encounters difficulties and challenges at least equal to those encountered by Timothy, and the clergy also need Paul's counsel and encouragement. Youthfulness and intimidating opposition tempted Timothy to compromise his stand on the truth of the Gospel, and pastors today may be tempted to water down their message lest it prove offensive to the different and powerful people they meet in their parishes. Paul here gives the answer to all faced with such temptations to discouragement or compromise: a reliance on the power and call of God and a constant ministry of teaching His Word. Clergy have access to a strength greater than their own. Through their ordination, the living God has called them to speak for Him and empowered them with His Spirit to perform this work. With undaunted courage, they must read the Scriptures to their flocks, feeding them on the Word of God, and apply that Word to their lives by their sermons and Bible studies. Only by fulfilling their God-given ministries and mandates to preach the Gospel can they save themselves (see 4:16). Like Paul, they have a call from God, and woe to them if they do not preach the Gospel (see 1 Cor. 9:16).

§X.   Various Age Groups (5:1–2)

> ఞ ఞ ఞ ఞ ఞ
>
> **5** 1 Do not strike out *verbally* at an elder *man*, but exhort *him* as a father; younger *men* as brothers,
>
> 2 the elder *women* as mothers, the younger *women* as sisters, in all purity.

Once again St. Paul urges his young colleague to embrace humility. Older men may look down on him and despise him for his youth (4:12), and may perhaps even sharply tell him to be quiet. Timothy might be tempted to respond to the **elder *man*** in kind and **strike out *verbally*** (Gr. *epiplesso*, lit., "to strike upon," to give him a tongue-lashing). Paul forbids this. Rather, Timothy must persevere in love to win over the offender, **exhorting *him*** as if he were his **father**, encouraging him to see the truth. He must lead his flock by example and not push his authority on them with sharp words. (Some scholars have suggested that Paul here discusses the issue of presbyters/elders, since he uses the Greek word *presbuteros*, the same word used in 5:17 to describe the clergy. However, Paul's use of the feminine term *presbytera* [elder woman] in v. 2, along with the references to younger women [Gr. *neotera*], suggests that in these present verses Paul uses the term *presbuteros* literally, to denote age, and not to denote clerical office.)

This family model must be applied to others in the church community as well. Timothy must relate to **younger *men*** as if they were his **brothers**, with affectionate camaraderie and love. **Elder *women*** must be treated as if each were his **mother**, with loving respect. Especially important is his relationship with the **younger *women***, to whom he must relate as to his **sisters**—that is, **in all purity**. The word "purity" (Gr. *agneia*) here has a sexual ring to it. Paul tells his younger colleague to take special care to observe every propriety, lest any hint of sexual scandal cloud his ministry.

St. Paul's use of a family model as the paradigm for relationships in the Church has as its common element closeness and love. The Church is not a club, a society, or a philosophy, in which each member keeps his own distance. It is a family—indeed, the family and house of God (3:15), in which each is bound to the others with indissoluble ties of spiritual kinship.

§XI.   Widows (5:3–16)

St. Paul addresses next another topic—the vexed question of the office of widow in the Church. These were not just any widows, women who had been bereaved of their husbands, but official church widows—that is, widows the church had put on its official list. In exchange for their ministry of solitude and prayerful intercession, the church supported them with food and lodging. Enrollment as an official widow involved a lifelong pledge of celibacy and commitment to a lifestyle of holiness. A generation or so later, St. Polycarp would write to the Philippians and describe the widows as "God's altar," the place of prayer. Widows were thus the visible embodiment of the Church's prayerful devotion to God.

However, some in Ephesus were abusing this noble office. Some widows were being supported who could well have been supported by their own families; other widows were being enrolled when they were young and later deciding to remarry, their pledge of celibacy notwithstanding; others still spent their time going from house to house—ostensibly to pray for the distressed, but also to spread gossip. The institution of church widows was in danger of falling into disrepute, and something needed to be done.

ॐ ॐ ॐ ॐ ॐ

3 Honor widows who are indeed widows.

4 But if any widow has children or grandchildren, let them first learn to show piety to *their* own house and to render a recompense to *their* parents, for this is acceptable before God.

5 Now she who is indeed a widow and who has become alone has hoped on God, and continues in the supplications and the prayers night and day.

6 But she who *revels in* luxury is dead *even* while she lives.

7 Order these things also, that they may be irreproachable.

8 But if anyone does not take forethought for his own, and especially for his own household, he has denied the Faith and is worse than an unbeliever.

Paul directs Timothy to **honor** (that is, support with church funds) **widows who are indeed widows**—that is, one who **has become alone** and desolate, one without any other support. Such a person has **hoped on God** as her only hope and so **continues in the supplications and the prayers night and day**. A true widow is thus a woman of prayer, being driven to this by her circumstances. Timothy should find and place on the official list women like these. But **if any widow has children or grandchildren** who can support her (a duty taken for granted in those days), then she is not alone or desperately reliant on God. Let the relatives of such a widow **first learn to show piety to *their* own house** and family, and **render a recompense to *their* parents** (that is, to the widow). This is the most elementary duty of piety. If the family will do this, they will be rewarded by God, for such support is **acceptable before God** and will bring His blessing on their house.

Timothy must take care that the widows he enrolls are **irreproachable** and women of prayer. If one *revels in* **luxury**, living a life given over to pleasure and ease (Gr. *spatalao*; compare its use in Ezek. 16:49 LXX), then she is spiritually **dead** even while physically alive. Such a widow should not be enrolled. Simple need is not the only requirement for being enrolled as a widow, since a church widow represents the Church. Timothy must **order these things** that the Church's high standards be upheld.

But what about the families who refuse to care for their widowed family members, but try to foist them off on the care of the Church? That person who **does not take forethought** and provide **for his own** dependents, especially if they are of **his own household** and family (such as his widowed mother or grandmother), that person has **denied the Faith** by his actions and is **worse than an unbeliever**. He must be cast out of the communion of the Church and excluded from the Eucharist. Thus Timothy must do all he can to ensure that widows are taken care of. The Church will care for the desolate ones (provided they are prayerful and of good repute) and pressure its families to care for their own widowed members.

୬ଡ଼ ୬ଡ଼ ୬ଡ଼ ୬ଡ଼ ୬ଡ଼

9 Let a widow be enrolled if she is not less than sixty years old, the wife of one husband,

10 witnessed to by good works, if she has brought up children, if she has welcomed strangers, if she has washed the feet of the saints, if she has aided the afflicted, if she has followed after every good work.

> 11 But reject younger widows, for when they become sensual in disregard of Christ, they want to marry,
> 12 incurring judgment because they nullified their first faith.
> 13 At the same time they also learn to be idle, going around to the houses, and not only idle, but also *accusing* gossips and busybodies, speaking things they ought not to.
> 14 Therefore, I intend younger ones to marry, bear children, rule their house, and give the adversary no opportunity to abuse,
> 15 for some have already turned aside after Satan.
> 16 If any faithful *woman* has widows, let her aid them, and let not the Church be burdened, that it may aid the ones who are indeed widows.

St. Paul then lists at length the criteria for enrolling widows on the official list, those who represent the Church. As well as being genuinely financially desperate, she must be **not less than sixty years old** and thus unlikely to remarry. She must be **the wife of one husband** and thus of stable character, not someone who has gone through several divorces and remarriages. She must be **witnessed to by good works**, having a reputation for piety. That is, she must have **brought up children** as a good mother and **welcomed strangers** into her home, being given to hospitality. As one involved in the Church's life, she must be one who **has washed the feet of the saints**—that is, welcoming Christians into her home. (Washing the feet of visitors was standard practice in those dusty days.) She must be one who has **aided the afflicted**, giving alms to the hungry. In fact, she must be one who has **followed after** and been devoted to **every good work**, someone always happy to do whatever she could.

Timothy must **reject younger widows**, however, by not putting them on the official list. In their first days of widowhood, they were happy enough to find solace in dedicating themselves to Christ in pursuit of celibacy and prayer. For many of them, though, that soon passes. The joys of prayer pale for them in comparison to other pleasures, and they soon enough **become sensual in disregard of Christ**. That is, despite their pledge of widowhood, they decide **to marry** again, even if it means that they **nullify their first faith** commitment to Him. Thus they incur **judgment** and condemnation by breaking their promise to Christ to serve Him perpetually as His dedicated widow.

Not only that, but these younger widows **also learn to be idle, going around to the houses** of the Christians, ostensibly to comfort the distressed, but in reality to find out the latest gossip and pass it on. Thus, as well as being idle, lazy, and useless (bad enough in itself), they are also *accusing* **gossips**, repeating things that are not true. They are **busybodies**, meddling in things that are none of their business, and **speaking things they ought not to**, whispering lascivious nonsense about who did what with whom.

These younger ones ought not to be on the list pledged to widowhood. Rather, Paul **intends** and directs (he uses the verb *boulomai*; compare its use in 2:8) for these **younger** widows to **marry, bear children**, and **rule their house** as contented and productive wives and mothers. (The domestic authority of women can be seen by Paul's choice of verb, the Gr. *oikodespoteo*, rendered here as "to rule a house"; women exercised a benevolent despotism in their homes.) If Timothy excludes younger unstable women from the official list, then the Church's **adversary**, who is looking for reasons to criticize, will have **no opportunity to abuse** and revile the Church. (It is crucial that Christians keep their behavior blameless in the world, for their adversaries are reviling loudly enough, and hostility to the Christians is growing.) **Some** widows **have already turned aside after Satan**, having given themselves over to pleasure (see v. 6), and have left the Church entirely, so Timothy must attend to this growing problem immediately.

Paul sums up by saying that the Church must care for true widows. If **any faithful** *woman* (that is, a woman believer) **has widows** in the family, **let her aid them** and support them. The Church's resources should be saved so that **it may aid the ones who are indeed widows**—the ones desolate and relying on God.

§XII. Elders (5:17–25)

ॐ ॐ ॐ ॐ ॐ

17 Let the elders who preside well be counted worthy of double honor, especially the ones toiling in *the* Word and in teaching.

18 For the Scripture says, "You shall not muzzle a threshing ox," and, "The workman is worthy of his reward."

19 Do not accept an accusation against an elder except on the evidence of two or three witnesses.

20 Those sinning, expose before all, that the rest also may be afraid.

21 I testify before God and Christ Jesus and the chosen angels that you keep these rules without prejudgment, doing nothing from partiality.

22 Do not lay hands quickly on anyone, nor share in others' sins; keep yourself pure.

23 (No longer drink water only, but also a little wine for the sake of your stomach and your frequent ailments.)

24 The sins of some men are quite plain, going before them to judgment, whereas others indeed follow after.

25 Likewise also, works that are good are quite plain, and the ones that are otherwise are not able to be hidden.

The apostle next deals with the topic of **elders** or presbyters (Gr. *presbuteros*), the local clergy of the Church, and he gives Timothy directions about how to relate to them. Some house churches were not sufficiently compensating the presbyters for their work; some other presbyters were indulging in open sin. Moreover, some of the laity, recently converted, desired to be ordained to the presbyterate. What is Timothy to do?

Paul first rules that the elders who **preside** and rule **well**, carrying out their tasks as leaders with competence, should be **counted worthy of double honor**. This is especially to be the case for the elders who not only preside liturgically, but who also **toil in *the* Word and in teaching**. Elders presided at gatherings of the Church, leading the prayers, organizing the communal life, settling disputes. They facilitated and guided the life of the community. Some of them not only did that, but also spent hours preaching and sharing the Gospel with inquirers (laboring "in the Word," Gr. *en logo*) and expounding the Faith to the believers (laboring "in teaching," Gr. *en didaskalia*). Timothy must see that such men receive "double honor."

What is this "double honor"? The "honor" in question is the same as for the widows (v. 3)—they are honored by being given money or donations in kind. Paul calls this honor "double" in the sense of being ample, just as Jerusalem was said to have received "double for all her sins" in that she received ample and full punishment for them (Is. 40:2). In the same way, the Church is to give the presbyters ample and sufficient reward for their work.

For those who resent this (perhaps those disgruntled with the presbyterate on account of the sins of some of its members?), St. Paul justifies it by two proverbs, one from the Old Testament **Scriptures** and the other from the oral tradition of Jesus' words. In Deut. 25:4, God commanded that the **threshing ox** not be **muzzled**. In those days, one separated grain by laying the freshly reaped stalks on the ground and leading one's ox to walk over them, dragging a threshing sledge over the stalks to separate the wheat from the chaff. The Law commanded that the ox not be muzzled or prevented from eating the newly threshed wheat as it worked. That is, it commanded men to show compassion for all, even for animals. In the same way, Paul says, the presbyters too must not work for free, but must be allowed to benefit from their labors. If an ox is to be compensated for its work, how much more an elder in God's Church?

The Lord Jesus said the same when He said, **the workman is worthy of his reward**. (St. Luke recorded this later in Luke 10:7.) That is, the laborer who works should not be deprived of his wages. When Jesus quoted this popular proverb, He applied it to the apostles He was sending out, saying they could justly accept whatever hospitality they were given. In the present context, Paul applies it to the presbyters—they too may justly be fed for their work. Thus, by quoting both the Old Testament Scriptures and the word of the Lord Jesus, Paul ensures that the clergy will be properly recompensed for their work.

The prominent position of the elders made them especially prone to accusation and complaint from those who felt slighted or excluded by their rulings or decisions. These discontented people would all too easily lodge **an accusation** of wrongdoing against that **elder**, possibly repeating some bit of slander heard making the gossip rounds. Accusations of sexual impropriety or financial embezzling would be easy to make, even when completely unsubstantiated. St. Paul therefore directs Timothy to **not accept** any formal accusation against one of the elders unless it is backed up by the solemn word of **two or three witnesses**. In this ruling, Paul simply follows the Law and age-old precedent (Deut. 19:15). Hearsay evidence and solitary gossip are not enough. To punish or depose a presbyter, one needs true and undeniable evidence. Otherwise, no presbyter would be safe from scurrilous and unjust slander; he would become the tool of the various cliques in the Church, powerless to rebuke sin.

If an accusation is substantiated, however, and the presbyter is **sinning** and persisting in serious sin (such as fornication or embezzling), then Timothy must **expose** such a man **before all** the Church, so that **the rest** of the presbyters also will **be afraid** to sin like him.

Because of the seriousness of these matters, Paul **testifies before God and Christ Jesus and the chosen angels** that Timothy **keep these rules without prejudgment** or favoritism (Gr. *prokrima*). He must not prejudge a charge against a presbyter, allowing personal friendship to sway him; he must not let **partiality** enter into the matter at all. God and Christ Jesus in heaven will see all, and the chosen angels who superintend order in the Church on earth and who are invisibly present will see as well. There can be no hiding from these, or from God's final judgment on the Last Day. Timothy must do all with an eye to this final judgment; he must not welcome a flimsy accusation against an elder he does not like, nor acquit a guilty elder that he favors.

The presbyteral office is fraught with spiritual danger. For this reason, Timothy must not **lay hands quickly on anyone** to ordain him to that office too soon, personal friendship notwithstanding. The would-be presbyter must be tested and allowed time to mature in the Faith. If Timothy ordains a man too quickly, this man will inevitably be puffed up by his newfound authority and fall into the judgment incurred by the devil (3:6). Timothy will then **share** in the other man's **sins** of office. This he must not do; he must **keep** himself **pure** from such offenses.

Paul then adds a quick parenthesis. Speaking of purity, he says, Timothy should not think that Paul is commending his current dietary practice as part of this purity! As a part of his asceticism, Timothy has been avoiding wine with his meals, abstaining from the beverage customarily drunk at all evening meals and **drinking water only**. Paul directs Timothy to do this no longer. Rather, he is to drink **a little wine** with his meals **for the sake of** his **stomach and** his **frequent** digestive **ailments**, for the wine will help him digest his food better. (The wine drunk in those days was diluted with two parts water to one part wine.)

After this quick personal aside, Paul returns to his topic of the perils of premature ordination. If Timothy *does* ordain too hastily, then sooner or later this will result in disaster. The **sins** and weaknesses of **some men** are **quite plain, going before them to judgment**, inviting God's judgment even in this life. Other sins are not so obvious and **follow after**, trailing behind the sinner. And this applies not just to sins, but to **works that are good** too: some of these are **quite plain**, so that we can see the goodness of a man as soon as we meet him, whereas the good works of other men are not so obvious. These works too, however, **are not able to be hidden**, but will be discovered later. Therefore, in order to discern whether a man is full of sins and weakness or full of good works, Timothy must wait and see. Eventually, he will see the candidate's true worth, and only then, when the candidate has proved himself worthy, should ordination take place. Timothy must proceed with patience and caution.

§XIII. Slaves (6:1–2a)

ॐ ॐ ॐ ॐ ॐ

6 1 Let all who are under a yoke *as* slaves esteem their own masters as worthy of all honor, lest the Name of God and the teaching be blasphemed.

2 And let not the ones having believing masters despise them because they are brothers, but let them serve *as slaves* to them all the more, because those who are helped by the kind deed are believers and beloved.

Having dealt with widows and elders, St. Paul turns to another group, that of the slaves. This was an especially delicate issue because many of the Christians were drawn from the slave ranks, and bad behavior from the Christian slaves would reflect badly on the whole Christian movement.

Therefore St. Paul directs that **all who are under a yoke *as* slaves** regard their masters as **worthy of all honor** and show them proper respect. If their masters are **believing** fellow-Christians, the slaves must not use that as an opportunity to **despise them** and be insolent. If people see Christian slaves disdaining their masters with impunity, they will conclude that the Christian Faith threatens the whole social fabric of that day, and **the Name of God and the teaching** of the Gospel will **be blasphemed**. Instead of treating their Christian masters with contempt, the Christian slaves should **serve *as slaves* to them all the more**, working even more heartily, since their masters **who are helped by** their **kind deeds** are fellow Christians, **believers** like themselves and **beloved** by God.

Some people in the secular world blame St. Paul (and the Church generally) for tolerating slavery and for urging the slaves to be obedient to their masters. They charge the Christian Faith with being oppressive and "nonprogressive" (the worst of sins by today's standards). What can be said in response?

First we must point out how revolutionary St. Paul was in actually addressing the slaves. Ancient writers exhorted the masters of the households to act in certain ways regarding their wives and their slaves, but it did not occur to them to exhort women and slaves as well. These latter groups they regarded as beneath them, as unteachable. The masters were the responsible ones. Unlike those writers, Paul accords the women and the slaves the same dignity as the freemen; he addresses the women equally with the men, the slaves equally with the masters. He does not regard the slaves as objects to be used and governed (albeit kindly), but as subjects with souls, as human beings answerable to God for their actions. We consider this to be self-evident, but that is only because we are heir to Christian teaching. The pagans had no such respect for their slaves.

Secondly, we must also point out that the Christian movement in the days of St. Paul was a small embattled minority in the midst of an increasingly hostile world. If society took the Christian Faith seriously, this would indeed spell the end of slavery—as eventually it did. But in the first century, for Paul to have emphasized the essential equality of all men and to have insisted upon the abolition of slavery would have politicized the Christian Faith and destroyed its mission. For then all the debates would have focused on the social issue of slavery, which most pagans accepted without a further thought and upon which the economy of the empire was based. All would have seen Christianity as essentially a social reform program, if not a clarion call for another slave revolt, and its true message would have been lost.

Paul knew that the true, timeless, and ultimately transforming message of the Church was not the abolition of slavery (or any needed social reform), but the forgiveness of sins and the healing of the human heart. In this salvation, the issue of slave or freeman was irrelevant, for the saved freeman was God's slave and the saved slave was a freeman in Christ (see 1 Cor. 7:22). To preserve the integrity of the Gospel, Paul needed to focus on its central proclamation of salvation through Christ and not rock the social boat prematurely. Everything would happen in its proper time (Eccl. 3:1)—including the conversion of the nations and the abolition of slavery. Paul knew that the task of his day was the preaching of the Gospel and the preservation of the Church.

§XIV. Opposition (6:2b–10)

ॐ ॐ ॐ ॐ ॐ

2   Teach and exhort these *things*.

3   If anyone teaches other *doctrines* and does not agree with healthy words, those of our Lord Jesus Christ, and with the teaching that accords with piety,

4   he is conceited, having understood nothing, but he has a diseased *craving* for debates and word-quarrels, from which come envy, strife, reviling, evil suspicions,

5   and constant irritation between men corrupted in *their* mind and deprived of the Truth, who suppose piety to be a means of gain.

As the apostle reaches the end of his directions to Timothy, he again tells him to **teach and exhort these *things***, meaning the principles enunciated throughout the epistle. In doing this, Timothy must beware of **anyone** who would contradict him and **teach other *doctrines*** or profess heterodoxy (Gr. *eterodidaskaleo*; compare its use in 1:3). Paul here refers again to those would-be teachers who specialize in "Jewish myths." Paul considers the teaching of these men to be *other* and heterodox because it **does not agree with healthy words, those of our Lord Jesus Christ**; it does not **accord with piety**. That is, it does nothing to promote spiritual health or lead one to value practical piety and holiness. Its sole result is to give people swelled heads and proud hearts, so that they are always spoiling for a fight. The self-promoting teachers who teach these things are no true colleagues of Timothy, and he must not regard them as allies.

Rather, Timothy must consider these men as the problem. For these teachers are **conceited** and blinded by pride (Gr. *tuphao*; compare its use in 3:6), and though they might claim spiritual insight, they actually have **understood nothing**. Having rejected the health-giving Word, they are spiritually **diseased**, as evidenced by their craving for **debates and word-quarrels**.

The word rendered "debates" (Gr. *zetesis*) can mean "investigations" (as in Acts 25:20), but here it means "controversies, arguments" (as in Acts 15:2). These men may claim to be interested only in investigating and discovering the truth, but actually all they want is the dark joy of a fight, of demolishing another's arguments and proving them wrong. The word rendered "word-quarrels" (Gr. *logomachia*) is connected with the Greek verb *machomai*, meaning to quarrel or fight (its use in Acts 7:26). These word-quarrels are simply delight in fighting over mere words. These problematic teachers are not concerned with actual issues or realities; they only want to show off and argue about verbal trifles.

Paul denounces this behavior as destructive, for out of it come **envy, strife, reviling, evil suspicions, and constant irritation**. That is, if Timothy leaves such men to do their work, all sense of community and harmony in the Church will be destroyed. The people in the church communities will be filled with envy one for another, will argue with each other when present and slander each other when absent. They will be filled with suspicion of each other's motives and never give each other the benefit of the doubt, constantly getting on each other's nerves. In short, the Church will become one big dysfunctional family, completely incapable of doing its work of imaging and making present the Kingdom of God.

Paul says that the **men** who produce such things are **corrupted in *their* mind and deprived** and robbed **of the Truth**. That is, these would-be teachers have lost their grip on the Gospel and now are incapable of seeing things as they really are. Their *mind* and spiritual focus is spiritually decayed so that they are now a dead loss (the verb "corrupted" is in the perfect tense, indicating a thorough and complete corruption). They even **suppose** that **piety** and the teaching office are **a means of gain**, for they want to become teachers for the financial gain they can get out of it. Paul warns Timothy about these men. Timothy must not humbly suppose them to be colleagues or allies. Rather, he must see their work for the threat it is and take action to oppose it.

৵ ৵ ৵ ৵ ৵

6 But piety with contentment is a means of great gain.

7 For we have taken nothing into the world, and we are not able to take anything out.

8 And if we have nourishment and shelter, with these we will be satisfied.

9 But the ones who desire to be rich fall into trial and a snare and many mindless and harmful lusts which sink men into ruin and destruction.

10 For the love of money is a root of all the bad *things*, and some by aspiring to it have been *completely* deceived *and led* from the Faith, and have pierced themselves with many a pain.

St. Paul's word in v. 5 about piety not being a means of gain leads him to a clarification. **Piety**, he says, is actually **a means of great gain**, provided that it is accompanied by **contentment**. The word translated "contentment" is *autarkeia*, a good classical word much-loved by the Stoics, meaning "self-sufficiency." A man who is *autarkes* has all he needs for happiness inside himself; he sits out of reach of the world's blandishments. The apostle says here that the teaching office can lead to gain—but only if one first renounces the scramble to grow rich and finds contentment within himself. The wealth of a teacher is a spiritual wealth, not a financial one.

Paul insists on the futility of hoarding wealth. For just as **we have taken nothing into the world**, being born with no possessions at all, so we will return to that state and leave with no possessions, for we **are not able to take anything out** of the world when we die. As the old proverb says, "There are no pockets in a shroud." Not, of course, that we should live in the same utter poverty in which we were born! We were born hungry and naked, but we must not live that way. We may pursue possession of **nourishment and shelter** (the nouns are in the plural), both meals and covering for protection. This *shelter* includes both clothing and a roof over our heads, for the Greek word used here, *skepasmata*, can mean both. If we have these, we **will be satisfied** and not torture ourselves to acquire more. In saying this, the apostle exhorts us all to simplicity. The basics needed for life may change and vary from culture to culture and from century to century, and what was found sufficient in first-century Rome may prove insufficient in twenty-first–century America. Nonetheless, the underlying principle is clear: Be satisfied with the basics, and regard anything more than food and warmth as a bonus.

One can see the wisdom of this when one examines the lives of those who **desire** and are determined **to be rich**. The word rendered "desire" (Gr. *boulomai*) conveys a sense of resolve and decision: those pictured here do not merely *want* to get rich; it is their consuming *ambition*. Such people **fall into trial** and temptation (Gr. *peirasmos*)—the fire of testing from which the Lord would have us delivered (see Matt. 6:13). Such men are caught in **a snare** and afflicted by **many mindless** and irrational **lusts** and desires. Those restless with the ambition to get rich find themselves enslaved to a multitude of inner desires, which all conspire to **sink men into ruin** and spiritual **destruction**. The **love of money** and passion for acquiring wealth dominates their whole life and fills their waking hours, eating up all their peace of mind and crowding out the love of God. It is **a root** and source **of all the bad** *things* in the world (Gr. *panton ton kakon*), for when this desire drives someone, there is no bad thing he will not contemplate in order to achieve his goal. Paul has known **some** who **aspired to** wealth in this way. They were *completely* **deceived** (Gr. *apoplanao*, used in Mark 13:22 for the deceiving of the elect) into wandering **from the Faith** and ended up having **pierced themselves with many a pain**. The relentless pursuit of wealth thus does not lead to joy, but to torment. The would-be teachers who flirt with this pursuit place themselves in great peril. Let Timothy himself beware!

§XV. Timothy to Flee Evil and Pursue Virtue (6:11–16)

> ॐ ॐ ॐ ॐ ॐ
>
> 11 But you, O man of God, flee from these things, and pursue righteousness, piety, faith, love, perseverance, meek-feeling.
> 12 *Strive in* contest *in* the good contest of faith, take hold of the eternal life to which you were called *when* you confessed the good confession before many witnesses.

In urging Timothy to beware the opposition, Paul concludes with a final and more positive encouragement. He addresses Timothy directly and emphatically, saying, **But you, O man of God**—*you* must live differently! (The *you* is emphatic in the Greek.) Paul urges Timothy not just to refrain from following the bad example set by those who desire riches and to **flee from these things** that they embody; he is also to actively **pursue** a life of holiness. He must not just run *from* sin; he must run *toward* holiness.

Thus he is to **pursue** and make progress in a life of **righteousness** and moral integrity, of **piety** and reverent devotion to God. He is to aim at **faith** (i.e. faithfulness and reliability; see Gal. 5:22), at **love** for his fellows, at **perseverance** under trial. He must work toward **meek-feeling** (Gr. *praupathia*), a commitment to meek and gentle responses no matter what the provocation. This is no easy undertaking, but involves vigorous action. Like a spiritual athlete, Timothy must *strive in* **contest** *in* **the good contest of faith**. The word translated "strive in contest" is *agonizomai*, which has echoes of the athletic games. It can mean to strive, to fight, to wrestle, and also to run a race, and it is cognate with the word *agon* (translated here as "contest" and in Heb. 12:1 as "race"). We can see the effort involved in this spiritual athleticism from our English derivative "to agonize." Timothy must pursue righteousness with all the effort of an Olympic athlete. (Though the Greek phrase here, *agonizou ton kalon agona*, can be translated "fight the good fight," I have not followed this translation, since Paul's usage of the word tends more to the athletic than the military; compare his use of the verb in 1 Cor. 9:25.)

Though such a striving for holiness is a matter of intense ascetic effort, it is this that will ensure that Timothy will finally **take hold of the eternal life** to which he was **called** when he was baptized. On the day of his baptism, Timothy **confessed the good confession** of faith **before** the **many witnesses**. He began well, promising to be faithful to Christ to the end. Now let him make good on that *good confession* of allegiance and *take hold* of the eternal life he was promised by living a life of righteousness. For only by living in holiness, as a true *man of God*, can he finally be saved. It is through our life of holiness as dedicated disciples of Christ that we seize the eternal life Christ offers us freely in the Gospel. If we do not pursue holiness and strive to live as Christ commands, that promise of life will slip through our fingers, leaving us empty and lost.

ॐ ॐ ॐ ॐ ॐ

13 I charge you before God, the One giving life to all things, and Christ Jesus, the One who witnessed before Pontius Pilate the good confession,

14 that you keep the commandment unstained, irreproachable until the appearance of our Lord Jesus Christ,

15 which He will show in its own times—the blessed and only Sovereign, the King of the ones *reigning as* kings and Lord of the ones *ruling as* lords;

16 who alone has immortality and dwells in unapproachable light; whom no one from men has seen or is able to see. To Him *be* honor and eternal strength! Amen.

Paul considers this to be so important that he again **charges** Timothy **before God** and before **Christ Jesus** that he **keep the commandment unstained** until the end. God is **the One giving**

life to all things, the transcendent Creator ruling above all, and He is able to care for Timothy in all his distresses. Christ Jesus is **the One who witnessed before Pontius Pilate the good confession** when He stood before him at His trial, confessing the truth regardless of the personal cost (Matt. 27:11), and He thereby gave Timothy an example of steadfastness before the authorities. By adjuring Timothy before God the Life-giver and before Christ the faithful Witness, Paul encourages him to trust in God's protection as he follows Christ's example. There may be trials to overcome as Timothy strives to keep the Gospel lifestyle **irreproachable** to the end, but God will not abandon him. Timothy must persevere. To do this, he must focus all his attention on the **appearance of our Lord Jesus Christ**. The word translated here "appearance" (Gr. *epiphaneia*) was used in ancient times to denote the arrival of a king into a city, as well as his accession to the throne. By using the word here to describe Christ's Second Coming, Paul stresses how that Coming will manifest all of Christ's royal authority and power when He comes again.

Timothy's trials may tempt him to doubt God's overruling power, but he must take heart. God the Life-giver rules over all. On the earth, men may strut about for now, wielding their little scepters, **the ones *reigning as* kings** and **the ones *ruling as* lords** (the words are participles from two verbs in the Greek, *basileuo* and *kurieuo*). But God is **King** and **Lord** above them all, and as the **blessed and only** One, the only true **Sovereign**, He will make all things serve His own purposes. He rules exalted far above our transient and fading existence. We all live for but a few years and then die; He alone is deathless, He **alone has immortality**. Far above this land of shadows, He **dwells in unapproachable light**. None on earth is the equal of Him, who is far above the eyes of sinful men. **No one from men has seen or is able to see** Him—much less thwart His purposes. Thinking of God's glory, Paul cannot resist crying out, **To Him *be* honor and eternal strength! Amen.**

Because God is exalted over all, **in its own times** and according to His own divine plan, He will **show** and manifest the appearance of Christ on the earth. Christ will come again, all in God's own time.

Meanwhile, Timothy may work hard, confident in God's overruling and providential purpose.

§XVI. The Rich (6:17–19)

ॐ   ॐ   ॐ   ॐ   ॐ

17 Charge the rich in this present age not to be high-minded or to hope on the uncertainty of riches, but on God, who richly gives us all things for *our* enjoyment.

18 *Charge them* to do good, to be rich in good works, to be generous and sharing,

19 treasuring up for themselves a good foundation for the future, that they may take hold of that which is life indeed.

Before his final charge to Timothy (in vv. 20–21), St. Paul inserts a word of instruction for him to pass on to those who are **rich in this present age**. (Perhaps mention of the greatness of God and the littleness of men in vv. 15–16 prompted him to bid Timothy to correct those who did not consider themselves so little!) He must **charge** and solemnly order the rich **not to be high-minded**. The Greek word here is *upselophroneo*, meaning "conceited." The rich are not to consider themselves as somehow above and exempt from the duties of common men. As Solomon noted ruefully, "The rich [man] answers roughly" (Prov. 18:23); the rich are tempted to think that they need not honor the image of God found in every man. St. Paul corrects such a notion, saying that the wealthy Christian (most of the rich of that day inherited their wealth) must avoid such arrogance and not treat others with high-minded contempt.

Also, the rich must not **hope on the uncertainty of riches, but** rather **on God**, the true and only source of wealth and security, who **richly gives us all things for *our* enjoyment**. Riches are simply a gift given from God. The One who *gives us all things*—the air, the sunshine, the rain—gave to the rich their wealth too, and the rich must focus their heart on Him, not on their money. Wealth is uncertain, for it can fail, being subject to ravages of moth and theft (and in our day, inflation and variations in the stock market!). The rich will find their only true security in God.

The rich must **do good** (Gr. *agathaergeo*, lit., "to work good things"), giving alms, liberating prisoners, building charitable institutions to care for the poor. Thus they will be rich not only in lands and gold, but also **in good works**. By being **generous and sharing** in this way, they will accumulate heavenly purses (Luke 12:33), **treasuring up for themselves a good foundation for the future**. Their alms and works of mercy will provide them with a good reward in the age to come, laying the foundation for their future blessedness. Thus they will **take hold of that which is life indeed**. The true life and security is the eternal life in the coming age, not the selfish spending on one's own pleasures now. We do not buy salvation, but rather use our money responsibly, as those who will one day be judged for it. God calls us to use mammon to do good in this age, that we might have an eternal welcome in the age to come (see Luke 16:9).

In the first century, a great gap yawned between the wealthy and everyone else, and though a middle or merchant class existed, it was not as large as it is in North America today. By first-century standards, those of the North American middle class are rich, and they should listen carefully to these words Paul addresses to the rich of his day. By global standards, a wealthy person may be defined as one who has the opportunity to eat breakfast, for many in the world have enough for only one meal a day. This does not mean that the middle class need feel guilty about their wealth (guilt rarely motivates one to enduring transformation), but they must recognize how wealthy they are. Christ teaches that the more wealth a man has, the more spiritual peril he has also, for to whom much is given, of him much is required (Luke 12:48). God gives riches as a stewardship and will demand a final accounting of how the wealthy man has used his wealth. Christ gives the general instruction to His disciples that they give their riches away and make purses in the Kingdom. Paul fills in the details of this instruction. The wealthy need not give away every penny they possess and live a homeless life on the street. But they must be generous and share all that they have, opening their hearts and their purses whenever they see a need.

§XVII. Timothy to Keep Safe the Deposit (6:20–21a)

ঙ৯ ঙ৯ ঙ৯ ঙ৯ ঙ৯

20 O Timothy, keep *safe* the deposit, turning aside from profane, empty-talk, the objections of what is falsely-named "knowledge,"

21 which some have professed and missed *the mark* concerning the Faith.

The apostle again returns to the final charge to Timothy he began in 6:13, repeating what he first said in 1:3–7. Paul addresses him by name, as **Timothy**, as if looking directly into his eyes for this final word. Timothy is to **keep *safe* the deposit** of the apostolic Tradition. The word rendered here "keep safe" is the Greek *phulasso* (cognate with *phulax*, or "guard"; compare its use in Acts 12:6). Timothy must guard the deposit of the Faith entrusted to him, keeping it secure as a guard would his charge. Paul describes this Faith as a "deposit" (Gr. *paratheke*) because Christ gave it to us once for all. The Christian Faith does not gradually unfold, and each succeeding generation does not discover or invent it for itself. The fullness of the Faith has already been given as a single body of Truth to the first-century apostolic Church. The task of each succeeding generation is to find life in it for themselves and then to pass it on whole and unimpaired.

ও EXCURSUS:
ON THE CHURCH'S THEOLOGICAL CONSERVATISM

The view that apostolic teaching is the deposit to be guarded explains the often-maligned theological conservatism of the Church. If the Church did not already possess the Truth, it would make sense for it to be "progressive" and open to changing its mind about what it previously believed. A scientist in his laboratory, for example, is always open to revising his previous theories and hypotheses because he does not yet know the scientific truth for which he seeks, and so he tries one theory after another until he thinks he has found it. But theological truth is not like scientific truth. Scientific truth is something we discover for ourselves, by our own powers and wisdom, and so we can never be absolutely sure we are correct. (Hence the so-called "paradigm shifts" in the scientific world.)

But theological truth is not discovered by our own powers. Christ our God revealed it to His apostles, and the apostles transmitted it to us. The teaching remains unassailable and unalterable because God has revealed it. The Church believes that it possesses God's absolute truth, and so it jealously guards it. The Church is not open to annulling its Tradition precisely because it believes it to be true. Why look for the truth when you already have it? Theological liberalism only makes sense if you do not have the truth but are still looking for it.

This does not mean that the Church disparages theological scholarship or finds no place for it in its life. Far from it! The Church has always nourished and valued scholars who examine, question, and plumb the depths of the Scriptures, teachers who discover and articulate the implications of the Faith. Men such as St. Gregory the Theologian, St. Maximus the Confessor, and St. Gregory Palamas come to mind. God gave His people a mind to learn new things as well as a heart to conserve old things, and we must use this mind to learn all we can in a spirit of humility. Treasuring the apostolic deposit and recognizing the finality of the Christian revelation therefore does not mean theological stagnation, much less obscurantism. But it does mean that all our investigations must recognize the truth of the teaching we already possess. We may learn more and add to what we already know; we may not unlearn and contradict the truth of what God has given us.

Timothy will be able to fulfill this charge and "keep safe the deposit" if he will **turn aside** from the **objections** and contradictions of the would-be teachers. These teachers promote their teaching as the latest in esoteric **knowledge** (Gr. *gnosis*), revealing the hidden things of the Law and the deeper truths of God, but it is **falsely-named**. It does not result in true knowledge of God at all, but is simply **profane** and sacrilegious **empty-talk**, worldly babbling, mere "room-noise" (Gr. *kenophonia*). Paul knows of **some** who **profess** such things and thereby **miss *the mark*** concerning the **Faith**, deviating from the straight path (Gr. *astocheo*; compare its use in 1:6). Let Timothy be warned, and let him use his teaching ministry to guard this apostolic deposit of truth!

§XVIII. Concluding Blessing (6:21b)

ॐ ॐ ॐ ॐ ॐ

21 Grace be with you.

In his final apostolic blessing, Paul widens his gaze, speaking not just to his beloved son Timothy, but also to all those who have been reading this epistle over his shoulder (as it were). The **you** is plural (Gr. *meth' umon*). Though addressing his words primarily to Timothy, he has the entire community there in his heart as well.

❧ St. Paul's Epistle to Titus ❧

Introduction

When Paul was released from his first imprisonment in Rome (probably about AD 62), it seems that he was accompanied by Titus (and Timothy?) as he left Rome. According to the surmises offered here, Paul made for his home in Antioch, sailing by way of Crete. This offered him an opportunity to make a quick evangelistic tour of the island en route. When he departed from Crete on the way to Antioch, he left his companion Titus there to finish up the work begun in haste.

Titus had a long history of working with St. Paul. He accompanied Paul and Barnabas when they went up to Jerusalem for the Council there in about AD 49 (Gal. 2:1). It would seem that he accompanied Paul and his companions on their third missionary journey. When Paul was in Ephesus, he sent Titus to Corinth to find out how the Corinthian church was faring; he was then to meet Paul again in Troas with the news. When Paul came to Troas, he did not find Titus there, and so went to Macedonia (probably Philippi; 2 Cor. 2:13; 7:5–6). When Paul found him there, he rejoiced at the news Titus brought and sent him back to Corinth bearing his Second Epistle to the Corinthians. After delivering the epistle, Titus was to help with the collection of money from the Gentile churches of the area and bring the money to the poor Christians of Jerusalem (2 Cor. 8:6, 16–24). Therefore, he was in Jerusalem when Paul was arrested.

Titus, then, was the confidant of St. Paul, so that Paul gave him many important tasks dear to his apostolic heart. Paul converted Titus early in his outreach to the Gentiles, and Titus became his true spiritual child (1:4). When Paul left Titus in Crete, he was leaving the island in the care of a seasoned colleague and a trusted friend.

Titus had much work to do in Crete. As well as ordaining elders for the various communities on the island, he needed to counteract the spread of false teaching, since many were promoting "Jewish myths" there just as others were doing in Ephesus (compare 1:14; 3:9). Further, Cretans were famous for their moral laxity (1:12–13), so that he needed to stress the practical aspects of piety and holiness. Titus' time there would not be wasted.

Yet, even so, Paul wanted Titus to return to him. The apostle planned to send someone to Crete to relieve him (either Artemas or Tychicus; see 3:12), and as soon as the relief arrived, Titus was to leave the island to meet his spiritual father Paul in Nicopolis, on the western shore of Achaia. After the weather became too bad for sailing, Paul would have to spend the winter in Nicopolis, and he wanted to have his dear Titus with him throughout that time.

Paul sent this epistle to Titus to help him finish up his task of ordaining elders in Crete and teaching the new converts there. He sent it possibly from Philippi, probably through the hands of Zenas the lawyer and Apollos (3:13), in about the summer of AD 62.

❧ The Epistle of St. Paul the Apostle to Titus ☙

§I.   Opening Greetings (1:1–4)

☙ ☙ ☙ ☙ ☙

1 1   Paul, a slave of God *and* an apostle of Jesus Christ, to further *the* Faith of *the* chosen of God and *the* real-knowledge of the Truth *which is* according to piety,

2   in the hope of eternal life, which the unlying God promised before ages of times,

3   but manifested in its own times *in* His Word, through the heralding with which I *myself* was entrusted according to the command of God our Savior,

4   to Titus, my genuine child in a common Faith: grace and peace from God *the* Father and Christ Jesus our Savior.

As with the first epistle to Timothy, Paul writes to Titus knowing that the epistle will be read also by others in the Cretan church, and so he writes with an eye to them as well (compare his final "Grace be with you all" in 3:15). This epistle functions therefore not only to instruct Titus in his ordering of the Cretan churches, but also to confirm his apostolic authority as given by St. Paul.

Paul begins by describing himself as a **slave of God** as well as an **apostle of Jesus Christ**. The self-designation of "slave" is unusual for Paul, for he customarily refers only to his apostolic office. By stressing his status as God's slave, Paul underscores his authority all the more, for this means that in all that he does, he is simply acting

81

on orders from his divine Master. The Cretans, known for their difficult personalities (compare 1:12–13), must hearken to what Paul—and therefore Titus, his delegate—has to say!

God did not give this authority to Paul for his self-aggrandizement. Rather, He gave it to him for the sake of the Church—**to further *the* Faith of *the* chosen of God and *the* real-knowledge of the Truth**. The words Paul will write are solely for the good of the Church, and his teaching will help them grow in the Faith and in the knowledge of the Truth. And not just any truth, but the Truth of the Gospel, which is not mere word-games (like the Jewish myths; compare 1:14), but rather is **according to piety** and results in a godly life. The word rendered here "real-knowledge" (Gr. *epignosis*) is a more intensive form of the word *gnosis*, or "knowledge." Paul's words to them will help them grow in an intimate knowledge of God, a recognition and deep experience of His saving Truth.

This faith centers on **the hope of eternal life**. By embracing it now, the believer can have the certitude of God's favor in the age to come. Moreover, Paul did not invent this Gospel message of eternal life himself. Rather, the **unlying God** (Gr. *apseude theos*) **promised** this **before ages of times**. That is, long centuries ago, He promised this very hope to His people Israel, speaking through His prophets (compare Rom. 16:25–26). And since He is the unlying God, the One who cannot lie but who is the Truth Himself, these prophetic promises must be fulfilled.

Now, Paul says, the time for their fulfillment has come, and this hope has now been **manifested in its own times** (that is, now, at the proper and appointed time). This hope is contained in God's **Word** and message and is conveyed to all people **through the heralding with which** Paul himself (the pronoun is emphatic in the Greek) was **entrusted**. Thus, Paul's words should be respected and obeyed, for through them the eternal God fulfills His prophetic promises to men. Paul says that he has been entrusted with this Gospel **according to the command of God our Savior**. Though it is possible that by "God" Paul refers to the Father, it is more likely that the title here refers to Christ. In the next breath he mentions "Christ Jesus our Savior" (v. 4), and he refers to Christ as the Savior in 2:13 (see notes on this verse). Along with the reference to Christ as "God our Savior" in 2:9, these verses show clearly Paul's belief in the full divinity of Jesus.

Since Paul, the herald of God, gives his instructions **to Titus**, the people must respect Titus as the recipient of this authoritative teaching. He is Paul's **genuine child in a common Faith**. That is, Titus is not only Paul's delegate, but his convert and beloved spiritual son. Since Paul and Titus hold the Faith in common, they stand together as equals. Paul may be the father, but both Paul and Titus work side by side before their common Lord. In writing to Titus, Paul bids him **grace and peace from God _the_ Father and Christ Jesus our Savior**. As in all Paul's opening greetings (see for example, Rom. 1:7; 1 Cor. 1:3; etc.), divine grace and saving peace come from the single divine source of the Father and the Son.

§II.   **The Need at Crete:**
       Titus to Order the Church (1:5–16)

ॐ ॐ ॐ ॐ ॐ

5   For this cause I left you in Crete, that you might set right the things that are lacking, and appoint elders in every city as I myself directed you:

6   if anyone is blameless, the husband of one wife, having children who have faith, and not accused of dissipation or insubordination.

7   For it is necessary for the bishop to be blameless as God's steward, not self-willed, not quick-tempered, not given to wine, not a striker, not given to shameful gain,

8   but hospitable, a lover-of-goodness, restrained, righteous, holy, self-controlled,

9   giving attention to the faithful Word which is according to the teaching, that he may be able both to exhort with the healthy teaching and also to expose the ones who contradict.

St. Paul begins with the main reason he **left** Titus **in Crete**—that he **might set right the things that are lacking**. Their time together was a whirlwind of activity, preaching the Gospel as God's heralds, with the result that many people repented and embraced the Faith. As regards the organization of the church communities, however, much remained to be done. Effective leadership was utterly lacking, and it was up to Titus to correct this situation. He must now go through the island again and **appoint elders in every city** as Paul himself **directed**. (The pronoun is again emphatic in the Greek: Paul stresses that this is an order coming straight from him, that Titus might meet less opposition as he carries out his work.)

Each house-church and community must have its own elder or presbyter (Gr. *presbuteros*). Titus must select men to ordain, looking for those with the right qualifications. Paul calls this officeholder a **bishop** (Gr. *episcopos*), since at this time the one office was described by both titles, "bishop" and "elder." It was only by the early second century that the terminology shifted, with the term "bishop" being then reserved for the leading elder alone, the focal point of leadership for each city and the main pastor.

Titus must find suitable leaders for the office. The candidate must be **blameless** and of good reputation. He must not be one who has been divorced and remarried, but must be of stable life and faithful character, **the husband of one wife** (see comments on 1 Tim. 3:2). His **children** must **have faith** and be believers themselves. They must **not** be **accused of dissipation or insubordination**. The word here rendered "dissipation" (Gr. *asotia*) denotes a reckless incorrigibility, the state of being lost beyond hope of saving. The pastor's children must not be insubordinate and rebellious like this, for their rebelliousness reveals a lack of loving wisdom on the part of the father who raised them. If their father was a man of good judgment, why then did his children rebel against his rule? And what might a church expect from such rule?

Moreover, the potential bishop or overseer of each house-church must have certain personal qualities of his own. He must be **blameless** and beyond reproach, since he is called to be **God's steward**. The term "steward" (Gr. *oikonomos*) denoted a servant assigned by the master and owner to have charge over all his house. The steward handled all the master's financial affairs and ran his whole house, exercising authority and making all the decisions. Such was the work of the pastor. God delegated to him the authority to run and manage His house. It was **necessary**, therefore, that he be blameless in his personal life.

The apostle then describes this blameless life. The candidate must **not** be **self-willed** or stubborn (Gr. *authades*), not ever insistent on doing everything his way. Similarly, he must **not** be **quick-tempered** or easily provoked (Gr. *orgilos*). He must **not** be **given to wine**, with a tendency to drunkenness (Gr. *paroinos*). He must not be **a striker** (Gr. *plektes*), one who lashes out when thwarted. He must not be **given to shameful gain** (Gr. *aischrokerdes*), one who might be easily bribed.

Not only must the presbyter-bishop be free of these disqualifying defects, he must have positive virtues as well. He must be **hospitable** (Gr. *philoxenos*, lit., "stranger-loving"), welcoming visitors from abroad into his home. He must be a **lover-of-goodness**. This Greek word, *philagathos,* describes one who delights in goodness, who instinctively withdraws from meanness and baseness, who rejoices to find the good in people. As well, he must be **restrained** (Gr. *sophron*) and prudent, able to act discreetly and patiently. He must be **righteous** (Gr. *dikaios*) and morally upright, **holy** (Gr. *osios*) and devout, **self-controlled** (Gr. *egkrates*), able to rein in his desires and master them.

He must **give attention to the faithful Word** of the Gospel, which was **according to the teaching** given by the apostles. That is, he must devote himself to the preaching of the Gospel as delivered to him by apostolic Tradition, avoiding the interpretations of false teachers. By concentrating his efforts on the apostolic Word, he will be **able** to fulfill his pastoral mandate. That mandate includes both **exhorting** and encouraging the faithful with **the healthy teaching**, leading them further on the paths of spiritual health and salvation, and also **exposing the ones who contradict**, the false teachers who would make trouble for the Church. By focusing on the Word, he will be able to deal effectively with both groups.

ॐ ॐ ॐ ॐ ॐ

10 For there are indeed many insubordinate ones, useless-talkers and deceivers, especially the ones of the circumcision.

11 It is necessary to stop-the-mouths of these, for they are overturning whole families, teaching what they ought not *to teach*, for the sake of shameful gain.

12 One of themselves, a prophet of their own, said, "Cretans are always liars, wicked beasts, idle bellies."

13 This witness is true. For this cause reprove them severely that they may be healthy in the Faith,

14 not paying attention to Jewish myths and commandments of men who turn away from the Truth.

15 To the clean, all things *are* clean, but to the ones who are defiled and faithless, nothing *is* clean, but both their mind and their conscience are defiled.

16 They confess *that they* know God, but by their works, they deny *it*, being abominable and disobedient and unapproved for any good work.

Titus needs to give such teaching, for **many insubordinate** and rebellious ones are circulating among the church communities looking to promote their own ideas, and the Church must be protected from them. Paul describes these rebellious teachers as **useless-talkers and deceivers**. The **ones of the circumcision**, the Jewish ones, are the worst. The word translated here "useless-talkers" (Gr. *matai-logos;* compare the cognate noun in 1 Tim. 1:6) denotes those whose words are useless and no good for anything, mere gas-bags. It is **necessary** to **stop-the-mouths** of these (Gr. *epistomizo;* compare the Gr. *stoma,* mouth), to shut them up—to "put a cork in it" (as we would say), overcoming them by reasoned argument. For **they are overturning** and ruining the faith of **whole families**, deceiving large groups of people, causing them to wander from the straight path of salvation. These teachers are teaching **what they ought not to teach**, promoting their teaching as deeper Christian truths when it is nothing of the kind. And this they do, not for disinterested love of men's souls, but **for the sake of shameful gain**, because they can collect money for teaching it.

Who were these teachers? It would seem that they were the Cretan version of what was being peddled in Ephesus as well—rabbinical "wannabes" who specialized in **Jewish myths** and allegorical interpretations of the Law. This explains why those of the circumcision were the worst—they promoted this with the most zeal because it involved their own ancestral Law. These teachers advanced all sorts of interpretations on each word of the Law, but none of it had anything to do with real holiness. Indeed, they were enslaved to sinful habits, having **turned away** from the apostolic **Truth** that called them to holiness. They obsessed over the minutiae of the Law and forbade this or that food as impure and unclean (compare 1 Tim. 4:3).

The truly **clean**, however, know that **all things *are* clean**, for what God wants now is the inner purity of the heart (Mark 7:18–19; 1 Tim. 4:4–5). But these men do not understand that, for they are not pure. Rather, they are **defiled and faithless**, and so to them **nothing *is* clean**, since they project their own internal uncleanness onto all created things. **Both their mind** with its moral focus and **their conscience**, which might have corrected them, are **defiled**, so how can they recognize the essential purity and goodness of creation? They **confess** that they **know God** and have access to His deeper truths, but **by their works, they deny *it***, their deeds giving the lie to their words. These men have proven to be **abominable and disobedient**, detestable to God, **unapproved** and worthless **for any good work**. These are no fit guides to holiness and salvation! The Christian presbyters must therefore work against their influence, striving by their own teaching to inoculate their flocks against it.

The people, alas, are particularly open to such false teaching. It is as **one of themselves** said, a **prophet of their own**: "Cretans

are always liars, wicked beasts, idle bellies." Scholars attribute the quote to Epimenides, a sixth-century BC philosopher with a reputation among the Cretans as a prophet. He also had, it seems, a flair for satire! But the world did not disagree with his prophetic denunciation of the Cretan national character. In fact the Greek word *cretizo*—to "Cretize"—meant "to lie." When Paul quotes one whom they regard as a prophet characterizing them as dishonest, malicious, uncivilized, shiftless, freeloading gluttons, he adds his own reluctant assent, saying, **This witness is true**. The stereotype, he says, proves accurate, and so Titus and his presbyters must **reprove them severely**, exposing their sin and sternly warning them that God insists on holy living. Let the Cretans pay no attention to their would-be teachers with their Jewish myths and their amoral version of the Faith. Only by heeding the stern reproof of Titus can the Cretans hope to be preserved safe and **be healthy in the Faith**.

§III.   Admonitions for Various Groups (2:1–15)

> ॐ ॐ ॐ ॐ ॐ
>
> **2** 1   But you, speak the things that are proper for healthy teaching.
>
>   2   Elder *men need* to be sober, reverent, restrained, healthy in their faith, in their love, in their perseverance.
>
>   3   Elder *women* likewise *are to be* reverential in demeanor, not slanderers, not enslaved to much wine, teachers-of-goodness,
>
>   4   that they may bring the young *women* to a sound mind *and* to be loving *to their* husbands, loving *to their* children,
>
>   5   to be restrained, pure, good home-workers, kind, submitted to their own husbands, lest the Word of God be blasphemed.
>
>   6   Likewise encourage the younger *men* to be sound-minded.

> 7 In all things show yourself to be a pattern of good works, with incorruption in the teaching, reverent,
>
> 8 healthy *and* uncondemnable in word, that the one from the opposing *side* may be shamed, having nothing base to say about us.
>
> 9 Slaves *need* to be submitted to their own masters in everything, to be well-pleasing, not contradicting,
>
> 10 not misappropriating, but showing all good faith, that they may adorn the teaching of God our Savior in all things.

After speaking of the Cretans' need to be "healthy in the Faith" (1:13) and of the inability of the "useless-talkers" (1:10) to meet that need, Paul tells Titus that it is up to him to restore the Cretans to health. **You**, he says (the pronoun is emphatic), must do the job and **speak** to them **the things** which are **proper for healthy teaching** and able to produce spiritual health. In directing Titus to exhort the whole church community to holiness, Paul focuses on several special groups.

He turns first of all to the **elder *men*** (Gr. *presbutas*). These must be **sober** (Gr. *nephalios*), maintaining an inner balance. This sobriety does not involve simply avoiding intoxication, but also keeping one's head and avoiding extremes. To be *nephalios* involves inner stability. Paul further exhorts his hearers to be **reverent** (Gr. *semnos*), noble and dignified; **restrained** (Gr. *sophron*), able to command respect through their modesty and self-control. The older men must be **healthy in their faith, in their love, in their perseverance**. These three nouns (*faith, love, perseverance*) are all preceded by the definite article, having here the force of *their* faith, love, and perseverance. That is, the older men must be spiritually healthy in their daily lives and not just in their doctrine. Their faithfulness to one another, their love for all men, their steadfast endurance of trial all must reveal their spiritual health.

Paul turns next to the **elder *women*** (Gr. *presbutidas*). These women must have the same virtues as their men, being **likewise** full of spiritual health. In particular, they are to be **reverential in demeanor**. The word translated here "reverential" (Gr. *ieroprepes*) is difficult to capture in all its nuances. It denotes the qualities that are proper (Gr. *prepes*) for worship in a temple (Gr. *ieron*), and it describes the demeanor one would expect from a priestess or temple attendant. The older women must live with the same reverence, stillness, and joy that one would exhibit in a holy place, for they too are engaged in the sacred duties of the home. As such, they must not be **slanderers** or malicious gossips (Gr. *diabolos*, elsewhere translated "devil"); they must not be **enslaved to much wine** and spend hours at the bottle. Rather, they must be **teachers-of-goodness** (Gr. *kalodidaskalos*), able to teach and promote goodness by their words and example.

Paul mentions one quality that the older women must share with the young women as well. (By "young women," Paul perhaps refers to newly married women; the Greek is *neas*, lit. "new ones.") That is, the older women must promote goodness through **bringing the young *women* to a sound mind**. The verb translated as "bring to a sound mind" is the Greek *sophronizo*, cognate with the word used in Mark 5:15 for the madman who was restored to his senses. The verb *can* mean simply to advise someone to be reasonable and sensible, but it seems more likely to have the stronger meaning here. Paul envisions the situation of younger women running home to their mothers after conflict with husbands and children, full of distress and despair. The older women are then to comfort them, to "bring them around," to encourage them to return and **be loving *to their* husbands** (Gr. *philandros*) and **loving *to their* children** (Gr. *philoteknos*), to take up once again their lives as wives and mothers.

Indeed, the older women are to inspire the younger to be **restrained** and self-controlled (Gr. *sophron*, compare its use in v. 2); to be **pure** and chaste (Gr. *agnos*, used here with sexual connotations as well). They are to be **good home-workers**. The word rendered "home-workers" (Gr. *oikourgos*) denotes industry in household matters. This is not just a matter of doing the housework, but rather includes total care of all domestic responsibilities, such as supervising servants and making business decisions. The young women also are to be **submitted to their own husbands**, not rebelling and overruling them, but following their godly lead. This is important if **the Word of God**, the Gospel they claim to follow, is not to be **blasphemed**, for a dysfunctional home is a bad advertisement for the Christian Faith.

Paul turns next to the **younger *men*** (Gr. *neoterous*) such as Titus himself. (Titus was perhaps thirty-three years of age.) These are to be **sound-minded** (Gr. *sophroneo*) like the young women, and not crazed with youthful zeal (or hormones!). Titus must provide himself as a **pattern** and example for them, that they might imitate his **good works**. He must show **incorruption in the teaching** he gives, so that his teaching and public demeanor exhibit no signs of being tainted by an unwholesome life; his life must be a model of moral integrity. He must be **reverent** and respectful (Gr. *semnotes*); **healthy *and* uncondemnable in word**, speaking only such things as no one could find fault with. Thus **the one from the opposing *side***, the pagans who watch them, will be **shamed** into silence, **having nothing base to say** about the Christians. Thus the Christians find their best defense of the Faith, not in eloquence and confrontation, but in a blameless and winning life.

Finally Paul turns to one other potentially problematic group, that of the **slaves**. They should **be submitted to their own masters in everything** and **be well-pleasing** to them. They must not be **contradicting** or argumentative, nor be **misappropriating**, pilfering when they are not watched. Rather, they must **show all good faith** in their work for their master, for this will **adorn the teaching of God our Savior**, commending it to all as something beautiful. There were many slaves among the Christian movement, and the world was watching to see what difference that Faith made in their lives—even as the world still watches all of us Christians today. (As mentioned in the notes on 1:3, the title "God our Savior" probably refers to Christ, not the Father. See also the notes on 2:13.)

ॐ ॐ ॐ ॐ ॐ

11 For the grace of God has appeared *as* salvation to all men,

12 disciplining us to deny the impiety and the worldly desires and to live restrainedly and righteously and piously in the present age,

13 anticipating the blessed hope and appearance of the glory of our great God and Savior Jesus Christ,

14 who gave Himself for us that He might redeem us from all lawlessness and cleanse for Himself a people *as His own* possession, zealous for good works.

15 These things speak and exhort and reprove with every *kind of* command. Let no one scorn you.

Paul now states the reason that slaves and all Christians (Paul here widens his view to include all the groups addressed in vv. 2–10) should "adorn the teaching of God" (v. 10) and lend it credibility through their good works: **the grace of God has appeared *as* salvation to all men**. That is, Christians should be concerned not to alienate those around them from the Gospel because, even though their neighbors are pagans, yet God has acted in Christ to save them as well. Our neighbor may be tyrannous and irritating, the worst of sinners, but we must see him as a brother whom Christ died to save, and live so as to make the message of this salvation credible to him.

The word rendered "appeared" (Gr. *epiphaino*) is cognate with the word rendered in 1 Tim. 6:14 and again here in v. 13 as "appearance" (Gr. *epiphaneia*). As said above, these words were used in ancient times to denote the arrival of a king into a city as well as his accession to the throne; by using them here, Paul speaks of Jesus the King as the embodiment of God's grace. Through Christ, God's reign of grace, mercy, pardon, and peace extends to all the world.

Receiving this grace and Gospel into our lives through baptism does not leave us unchanged, but begins to transform us. The Gospel teaching we accepted is **disciplining us** and training us to war against the passions. (The word translated "discipline," Gr. *paideuo*, is the word used for the correction fathers give to their sons; compare Heb. 12:7.) Thus, adherence to the Gospel involves ascetic self-discipline and determined resistance to the passions. The Gospel trains us **to deny the impiety and the worldly desires** that rule this self-indulgent age and **to live restrainedly and righteously and piously in the present age**. Children of this age live with unrestrained license, indulging the passions; they walk unrighteously, caring little for honesty; they live impiously, caring nothing for the duties of the devout or the demands of religion. But those who have welcomed God's grace and the Gospel teaching live with restraint, righteousness, and piety, as strangers and aliens in this present age, since they are **anticipating the blessed hope**, the **appearance of the glory of our great God and Savior Jesus Christ**. Though living in this world, they belong even now to the world to come, and their hearts always look to the horizon for the appearance (Gr. *epiphaneia*) of Christ, who will come in the royal glory of the Father to reign forever.

We note that St. Paul refers to Jesus as the "great God and Savior." This is unusual, for Paul rarely refers to Christ as "God," usually reserving this designation for the Father (compare 1 Cor. 15:24, 28). Though it is grammatically possible (as the RSV mentions in a footnote) to translate this phrase as "the appearance of the great God and our Savior Jesus Christ," so that "God" describes the Father and "Savior" describes Jesus Christ, it seems clear enough that Paul here uses both terms, "God" and "Savior," to refer to Jesus Christ. It is the uniform teaching of the New Testament that the blessed hope involves the coming of Christ, not of Christ and the Father as well. The title "God and Savior" is drawn from the world of Hellenism, whose kings (such as the Ptolemies) styled themselves gods and saviors. Jesus Christ, says St. Paul, is the only real God and Savior, the only true King, and our allegiance is to Him alone.

This present verse is therefore one of the clearest assertions in the New Testament of the full deity of Jesus of Nazareth. It does not, however, represent any development or change in Paul's thinking, for even in the earlier prison epistle to the Philippians, Paul had written that Christ "was in the form of God" (Phil. 2:6). Paul here uses the strongest language possible, applying the divine titles "God" and "Savior" to Jesus in order to stress His transcendent glory. Christ will come with a glory previously unknown in this age, and it is by this glory that He calls us to remain unspotted and holy while we live in the midst of it. Only by looking to the immeasurable glory that Christ will reveal to us when He comes can we discipline ourselves now with regard to our worldly desires. Christ's divine glory forms the counterbalance to the fading glory of this age and helps us resist its lure.

The One who will come in glory is the very One who **gave Himself** for us, dying on the Cross, **that He might redeem us from all lawlessness** and from the moral chaos that characterizes this age. Formerly, we were in bondage to our sins, but Christ's death set us free. In baptism, Christ **cleansed** us **for Himself** so that now we belong to Him, as **a people** for *His own* **possession** (compare Ex. 19:5). Formerly we were zealous for sin, indulging every passion without restraint, but now we are **zealous** only for **good works**. Since the Gospel teaching we have accepted involves such a change in life, how can the slaves (and all those in Crete) not take care to "adorn the teaching" (v. 10) of the Gospel by their holy lives?

St. Paul concludes by directing Titus to **speak** and insist on the things outlined above to all in Crete. He is to **exhort** and encourage them; he must **reprove** and expose sin **with every *kind of* command** and with all the authority he can muster, and **let no one scorn** him or push his words to one side. Titus stands among them with the fullness of Paul's authority—he must not be afraid to use it!

§IV.　General Admonitions (3:1–7)

ॐ ॐ ॐ ॐ ॐ

3 1　Remind them to be submitted to rulers, to authorities, to be obedient, to be prepared for

> every good work,
> 2 to slander no one, to be not quarrelsome, *to be* forbearing, demonstrating all meekness to all men.

St. Paul next gives a series of general admonitions that Titus must pass on to all his flock. Paul gave this basic Christian teaching to them when they were first converted, but Titus still needs to **remind them** of it, given their rough national character (see 1:12–13). (The Cretans are not alone in the ability to benefit from periodic reminders and encouragement to holiness!)

In particular, Titus's flock are **to be submitted to rulers** of regions and cities and to all the local **authorities** and civic officials. They are **to be obedient** to them and **be prepared** and eager to undertake **every good work** and duty that may be required of them. They are **to slander no one**, even though the secular world might slander them as Christians. They must **not** be **quarrelsome** (Gr. *amaxos*) and must refuse to fight back even when provoked, being **forbearing** and yielding when confronted, **demonstrating all meekness to all men**. That is, in all situations, they must be gentle, controlling their tempers and harnessing their inner strength.

Paul wants his Cretan converts to exhibit such good civic behavior, for the world is watching the Christians closely and forming judgments about the new movement. If the Gospel is to spread, the world must see that conversion to Christ improves one's character, taming wildness and making the converts more productive members of society. More than simply being concerned for the salvation of the souls of his flock, Paul is concerned for the salvation of the world.

> ॐ ॐ ॐ ॐ ॐ
>
> 3 For we *ourselves* also once were mindless, disobedient, deceived, enslaved to various lusts and pleasures, spending *our time* in wickedness and envy, abhorrent, hating one another.
> 4 But when the kindness of God our Savior and His love-for-man appeared,

> 5 He saved us, not from works which we *ourselves* did in righteousness, but according to His mercy, through *the* washing of regeneration and renewal in *the* Holy Spirit,
>
> 6 whom He poured out upon us richly through Jesus Christ our Savior,
>
> 7 that being justified by that One's grace we might become heirs according to *the* hope of eternal life.

As incentive for the Cretans to be forbearing to those pagans who challenge them, Paul recalls their own pasts. The pagans who confront them may be stupid and worthless—but they used to be like that themselves! They should remember that and have a little patience with those who now provoke them. Indeed, St. Paul includes himself in this category of stupidity and sinfulness. "We too," he says (the pronoun is emphatic in the Greek), "were exactly the same way!" Prior to their conversion to Christ, they too were all entangled in the same net of sin. They were **mindless**, with no spiritual insight at all (Gr. *anoetos*, not having any *nous*, or mind). They were **disobedient** to all of God's moral commands and **deceived** by the devil, not perceiving that they were on the way to destruction. They were **enslaved to various lusts and pleasures**, addicted to internal desires and external things such as sex and stimulants. They passed all their time in useless frivolities, wallowing in their **wickedness** and sinful indulgence, enslaved to an **envy** of others' pleasures which would not let them rest even then. And there was thus no camaraderie with other sinners, no honor among thieves or loyalty to their fellows. Each had a swollen ego in competition with the others. Each person was **abhorrent** and despicable; all of them spent their time **hating one another**, filled with anger. Can the Cretan Christians not remember how they used to be?

Looking back on their sinful past only throws into greater prominence how God has so wonderfully saved them from it. For **when the kindness of God our Savior and His love-for-man**

(Gr. *philanthropia*) **appeared** in the Person of Christ, God **saved us**, forgiving and transforming us, breaking the shackles of the sins that bound us and setting us in this new life of righteousness. Obviously, this was **not from works which we *ourselves* did in righteousness**, for we *had* no such works! Rather, it was **according to His mercy**, freely pardoning us sinners when we had no defense to offer for our sins. It was **through *the* washing of regeneration and renewal in *the* Holy Spirit**.

For that is what God did for us in Holy Baptism. Our baptismal washing bestowed a spiritual regeneration and rebirth, and (through the baptismal laying on of hands and holy anointing) an ongoing life of renewal in the Holy Spirit. The word translated "regeneration" (Gr. *paliggenesia*) is used in Matt. 19:28 to denote the age to come, for in baptism we receive now as individuals the power that will one day give birth to the new world. Thus baptism begins a life of constant "renewal" (Gr. *anakainosis*; compare its use in Rom. 12:2) and ongoing transformation of our minds and attitudes. It is through this baptismal experience that God saved us, separating us from our old sinful lives and putting into our hearts the life-giving power that one day will give birth to a new world.

God offers this experience to all willing to make a break with their sinful past. For God **poured out** His Holy Spirit upon the Church **richly** and abundantly **through Jesus Christ our Savior** on the Day of Pentecost, and since that day, the Spirit has been available to all. (The verb translated "poured out," Gr. *ekexeen*, is in the aorist tense, denoting a past, once-for-all experience—a reference to the definitive Day of Pentecost; compare its use in Acts 2:33.)

Now all can be **justified** and forgiven **by that One's grace** (Gr. *te ekeinou chariti*, a stronger form than "by His grace"; the emphasis is on that One who alone can save us). And this forgiveness is not the final goal. The end is more glorious still: we are to **become heirs** of God's Kingdom and of all His boundless riches on the Last Day. Thus we cling to this **hope** and certain promise of **eternal life** in the age to come, which beckons us home and gives us the incentive to persevere in righteousness.

⊗ EXCURSUS:
ON THE TERMS "GOD OUR SAVIOR" AND "APPEARANCE"

St. Paul uses these terms very often in this short epistle. We find the term "God our Savior" or "Christ our Savior" in 1:3, 4; 2:10, 13; and 3:4, 6, and the word "appearance" or its cognate "appear" in 2:11 and 3:4, as well as in 1 Tim. 6:14; 2 Tim. 1:10; 4:1, 8. Why does Paul favor these terms so heavily in these pastoral epistles?

I would suggest that Paul uses these terms so much in these later epistles out of his concern to defend the true lordship of Christ against the many rivals. The term "savior" (Gr. *soter*) designated divinity for the ancients, and they used it to describe both gods and men. By using this term so extensively, Paul stresses that in God and His Christ alone reside true divinity, lordship, and salvation. All others claiming the title are pretenders and not capable of saving their devotees at all. Similarly, the words "appearance" (Gr. *epiphaneia*) and "appear" (Gr. *epiphaino*) were used to describe the coming of a king and his accession to the royal throne. In his use of the term, Paul insists that Jesus is the only true King, and His Kingdom—revealed in this age as a *mysterion* (or mystery) for the initiated and consummated in fullness at His Second Coming—is the only real Kingdom. All other human kingdoms and sovereignties are phantoms and doomed to fade.

I would further suggest that Paul's experience of imprisonment and trial helped sharpen his recognition of these truths. Throughout his imprisonment, Paul had time to reflect on Rome's authority and on the power of Caesar, the king of the world. This allowed the apostle to appreciate anew the authority and power of Jesus, the true King of the World and Ruler of the age to come, whose Kingdom would eventually swallow up and supplant all the failing kingdoms of this age (Rev. 11:15). It is this renewed appreciation for the

> divine Kingship of God and His Christ that we see reflected
> in the special vocabulary of these later epistles.

§V.   Titus to Act with Confident Authority (3:8–11)

> ॐ ॐ ॐ ॐ ॐ
>
> 8 Faithful *is* the word, and I intend you to insist
>   concerning these things, that those who have
>   had faith in God may be mindful to preside
>   over good works. These things are good and
>   profitable to men.
> 9 But stand-back from foolish debates and gene-
>   alogies and strifes and quarrels *about the* Law,
>   for they are unprofitable and useless.
> 10 Reject a factious man after a first and second
>   admonition,
> 11 knowing that such a one has been perverted
>   and sins, being self-condemned.

Paul begins to sum up his directions to Titus, assuring him of
the reliability of the promise of final reward. **Faithful *is* the word**
that promises this, and his Cretan flock must walk in righteousness
if they would inherit the reward. Paul **intends** and counsels Titus to
insist and speak confidently about these things. The word rendered
"intend" (Gr. *boulomai*; compare its use in 1 Tim. 2:8) shows that
Paul does not simply wish Titus would do this; he orders him to do it.
For Titus's authoritative insistence is necessary that **those who have
had faith** and are believers **be mindful** and careful to **preside over
good works**. The word rendered "preside over" (Gr. *proistemi*) is used
in 1 Thess. 5:12 to describe the work of the presbyters. As presbyters
have the responsibility to care for their flocks, so all Christians have
the responsibility of doing good works and must diligently attend
to their task. Such works include almsgiving, visiting the sick, and
offering hospitality to strangers.

Titus should insist on **these things** (that is, Paul's instructions outlined in this epistle), for they are **good** and pleasing to God as well as **profitable to men**. But Titus must **stand-back** and have nothing to do with the **foolish debates** of the would-be teachers of the Law, with all their **genealogies** and absurd interpretations (see 1:14). These are **unprofitable** to men and **useless** for the work of sanctification. They lead only to **strifes and quarrels** over their interpretations of the **Law**. (The words translated "strifes" and "quarrels" are both plural in the Greek; the image is one of fight after fight.) If Titus wants to speak things truly "profitable to men," he should avoid these!

Some in the church may refuse Titus's instructions, and he must deal severely with them. If such a one refuses to accept his correction and confrontation, Titus must warn him again. But if such a one continues his work of teaching harmful things, Titus must expel him from the communion of the Church and deny him entry to the Eucharist. He must thus **reject** such a **factious man after a first and second admonition**. It will be no use to warn him further, for he **has been perverted** in his thinking and is unable to profit from further admonition; he **sins** and rebels against God willfully, being **self-condemned** and guilty, condemned by his own stubbornness.

The word translated "factious" is the Greek *airetikos*, from which the English word "heretical" comes. It is cognate with the Greek word *airesis*, or "faction" (compare its use in Gal. 5:20, where it describes divisive cliques in the church). Originally the word *airesis* meant any choice, whether sinful or not, and was cognate with the verb *aireo*, "to choose"; but it came to mean preferring one's own opinion in defiance of others, creating divisive factions. In the Church it came to mean standing apart from the Church's received Tradition—heresy in the strictest sense. Paul uses the term with this latter meaning. The "factious man" he refers to is the stubbornly divisive man, the one who accepts no admonition. He is a heretic, not so much because he espouses incorrect doctrine, but because he proudly refuses the Church's authoritative correction. The emphasis is not on the content of his doctrine, but on the state of his heart.

§VI. Final Admonitions (3:12–15a)

> ৵ ৵ ৵ ৵ ৵
>
> 12 When I will send Artemas or Tychicus to you,
>   be diligent to come to me at Nicopolis, for I
>   have decided to winter there.
> 13 Diligently send forth Zenas the lawyer and
>   Apollos that nothing may be lacking for
>   them.
> 14 And let our own *people* also learn to preside
>   over good works to *supply* necessary needs,
>   that they may not be unfruitful.
> 15 All who are with me greet you. Greet the ones
>   who love us in *the* Faith.

Paul concludes his epistle with some personal matters. He **will send Artemas or Tychicus** to Titus to relieve him in Crete. (It seems that Paul is not yet sure which one he will send; perhaps whichever one arrives first and is willing to travel to Crete.) When these arrive, Titus must **be diligent to come** to Paul at **Nicopolis** on the west coast of Achaia. Paul has **decided to winter there** and wants to have his dear colleague Titus with him throughout that time. As for **Zenas the lawyer and Apollos**, the ones who brought Paul's epistle to him, Titus is urged to **diligently** and eagerly **send** them **forth** on their journey with all they need, that **nothing may be lacking for them**. Let these be sent off to continue their journey, fully provided with the food and money they will require. Zenas was probably a Roman jurist; though the term "lawyer" may also designate an expert in the Jewish Law, this is less likely. Apollos was Paul's well-known Alexandrian colleague (see Acts 18:24–28; 1 Cor. 3:5–6).

The resources to help these men will of course be supplied by the Cretan church. They have the duty and joy to provide for such men as Zenas and Apollos—and not just for them. Let Paul's and Titus's **own *people***, the Cretan Christians, **learn to preside over good works to *supply* necessary needs** for others as well. (The word rendered "preside over" is the Gr. *proistemi*, used in v. 8 to describe their busy devotion to such works.) The Cretan church must delight to meet the necessary and pressing needs of any who require their help. By doing this, they will **not be unfruitful**, but will bear fruit for the glory of God by helping others in the world.

Paul ends, in good epistolary fashion, by passing on the greetings of **all** the Christians who are with him (possibly, as we have suggested, in Philippi). Titus in turn must **greet** on Paul's behalf **the ones who love** them **in *the* Faith** there in Crete. The verb rendered here "love" is the Greek *phileo*, cognate with *philos*, or "friend." Paul extends his Christian greeting of peace to those who are his friends in Christ. Though he may not know them very well (after such a quick tour of Crete), yet in the Faith they are his true and beloved friends. They may be of a different nation; they may be Gentiles and far from Paul's ancestral Jewish roots. But because they share the same Faith and the same Lord, they are still Paul's *own people*, and he is one with them.

§VII. Concluding Blessing (3:15b)

ॐ ॐ ॐ ॐ ॐ

15 Grace *be* with you all.

Paul adds his final word, doubtless written in his own hand as a sign of authenticity (compare 2 Thess. 3:17). Mindful of those of Titus's flock reading the epistle over his shoulder (as it were), Paul concludes with a blessing of **grace** upon them **all**. His blessing is not just for Titus, but also for all to whom he ministers.

❧ St. Paul's Second Epistle to Timothy ❧

Introduction

This epistle was written from Death Row. Paul had been arrested again (probably, as we have suggested, when he visited Ephesus in the spring of 65). We do not know the circumstances of this arrest. We may suppose, however, that it produced great trauma. Paul writes in 1:4 of Timothy's tears (possibly shed as the Roman soldiers led Paul away?) and in 1:15 of all in Ephesus and the surrounding province of Asia deserting him (possibly running for cover themselves?). Whatever the circumstances, Paul at length found himself back in prison in Rome. He had, it appears, a preliminary trial of sorts (4:16) and now faced the final mile of his journey. He knew that his imprisonment would end in his execution. There was no possibility of release. Death was imminent. As a Roman citizen, he could not be crucified. Instead, he faced death by beheading.

It was in this situation that he wrote again to his beloved spiritual child Timothy in Ephesus, asking him to come to him in Rome as soon as he could. He knew that soon he would not be there to advise and encourage him. But though Paul would soon end his earthly pilgrimage, Timothy still had many miles to go. The weary apostle therefore wrote to his young friend one last time to encourage him and brace him for the struggle. It was to be his final testament to Timothy and to the Church.

And though it was written from the very shadow of death, the epistle still breathes an atmosphere of hope. Paul does not think only of his own fate, but of the necessary tasks Timothy must undertake. Paul looks not inward to his own suffering, but outward to the on-going work of the Church. For his own part, he is content. He knows that he has kept the Faith and that his reward awaits him (4:7–8). His concern and heart lie entirely with Timothy and the Church.

Paul wrote this Second Epistle to Timothy from Rome, probably in the late summer or early autumn of 65. In the following June (as we suggest) he was beheaded with the sword. Paul took the Lord's Name before the Gentiles and kings and before the sons of Israel, suffering for His sake (Acts 9:15–16). The apostle to the Gentiles fulfilled his great apostolic task and entered into the joy of the Lord. Through his prayers, may we fulfill ours as well, and follow him into the Kingdom!

❧ The Second Epistle
of St. Paul the Apostle to Timothy ❧

§I. Opening Greetings (1:1–2)

❧ ❧ ❧ ❧ ❧

1 1 Paul, an apostle of Christ Jesus by *the* will of God according to *the* promise of life in Christ Jesus,

2 to Timothy, *my* beloved child: grace, mercy, *and* peace from God *the* Father and Christ Jesus our Lord.

As is his custom, Paul stresses his authority as **apostle**, saying that this came **by *the* will of God** when he was knocked to the earth on the road to Damascus. Even in his final hours, sitting in the shadow of death, Paul has never forgotten his apostolic calling, and that the will and plan of God rules his life. God bestowed his apostolate upon Paul **according to *the* promise of life in Christ Jesus,** and even though facing certain death, Paul thinks only of the eternal life God has promised him as the disciple of Christ Jesus.

He writes to Timothy as to his **beloved child** and spiritual son. To his usual greeting of **grace** and **peace** (compare 1 Cor. 1:3; Gal. 1:3; etc.) he adds the blessing of God's **mercy**. This is unique to his epistles to Timothy. Timothy has a special place in Paul's heart, and as he thinks of the magnitude of the task facing his young protégé, he prays that the divine mercy will be upon him as well.

§II. Opening Thanksgiving (1:3–5)

❧ ❧ ❧ ❧ ❧

3 I thank God, whom I worship with a clean conscience *as did* my forefathers, as I unceasingly

---

> have the remembrance of you in my prayers
> night and day,
> 4 longing to see you, as I remember your tears,
> that I may be filled with joy.
> 5 For I have received a reminder of the unhypo-
> critical faith *which is* in you, which dwelt first
> in your grandmother Lois and your mother
> Eunice, and I am persuaded that it is also
> in you.

In the opening thanksgiving customary in epistles, Paul **thanks God**, whom he **worships with a clean conscience**. The word translated "worship" (Gr. *latreuo*, cognate with *latreia*) is the word used for the sacrificial worship of the temple; compare its use in Rom. 9:4. St. Paul uses this verb to refer to the liturgical worship of the Church, for the Church offers the true Sacrifice. Though the world has condemned Paul as a criminal, Paul knows that he is innocent, and he affirms that he serves God with a clean conscience. Behind this protestation stands the slander of his unbelieving Jewish adversaries, who accuse him of being an evildoer and an apostate from the Law, and for whom Paul's sentence of death represents the judgment of God. "On the contrary," Paul replies, "I have maintained a clean conscience all my life and serve God with the same integrity as **my forefathers!**" Paul is no apostate from the Law, but stands in a long line of God's devout servants.

From his prison cell, Paul **unceasingly** makes **remembrance** of Timothy in his prayers before God, praying for him **night and day**. When Paul arises to pray at night and when he stands to pray in the day, he has Timothy and his ministry on his heart and on his lips. Even now he **longs to see** him, and the **tears** his young friend shed (probably at Paul's arrest) feel like a dagger through his heart. If only he could see Timothy one more time, he would be **filled with joy**.

As it is, Paul has **received a reminder** of him. The word translated "a reminder" (Gr. *upomnesis*) is the word used in 2 Pet. 1:13; 3:1, where it refers to Peter's epistle itself. Paul has received something concrete that has brought Timothy to his memory again. What was it? I would suggest that it was a letter to Paul from a now-unknown sender in which Timothy and his struggles in Ephesus were mentioned. Perhaps the writer of the letter mentioned how Timothy felt embattled in his ministry, but still strove to carry out his apostolic mandate.

Paul encourages Timothy by commending him for his **unhypocritical faith**, which refuses to be intimidated. He mentions that such a courageous faith **dwelt first** in his **grandmother Lois** and his **mother Eunice**. We know little about these women, only that Eunice was a Jewish woman married to a pagan Gentile (Acts 16:1). Perhaps both women were Jews married to pagan husbands? If that is so, it would explain why St. Paul singles them out for mention—they are examples for Timothy of persevering faith in the midst of difficult circumstances. By mentioning them, Paul encourages Timothy to follow in their steps and persevere in his faith regardless of the difficulties. In fact, Paul says, he is **persuaded** that such a dogged determination and faith dwell in Timothy too.

§III.   Timothy to Preserve the Faith by God's Power (1:6–14)

ૐ ૐ ૐ ૐ ૐ

6   And for this cause I remind you to rekindle the spiritual gift of God which is in you through the laying on of my hands.

7   For God has not given us a spirit of cowardice, but of power and love and sound mind.

8   Therefore do not be ashamed *at all* of the witness of our Lord, nor of me His prisoner, but suffer hardship with *me* for the Gospel according to *the* power of God,

Mention of Timothy's family heritage of piety leads Paul to encourage him in his ministry. Since that faith dwells in him too, let him **rekindle** that *spiritual* **gift of God** (Gr. *charisma*) which he received at his ordination **through the laying on of** Paul's

hands, that its fire may illumine him in the dark days to come. The weight of ministry is falling heavily on Timothy's young shoulders: his spiritual father and mentor awaits execution in Rome, opposition mounts in Ephesus, more persecution looms on the horizon. Timothy may be tempted to give up, and Paul wants to encourage him. Timothy comes from a long line of God's faithful servants—let him be bold! He must not let the flagging flame of faith go out—let him rekindle and fan into a flame the gift given him and fight on! The Holy Spirit given him at ordination does not result in **cowardice** (compare Rom. 8:15). Rather, the Spirit of God fills him with **power and love and sound mind**.

This last word, rendered here as "sound mind" (Gr. *sophronismos*), has echoes of moderation, prudence, and self-control. By the Spirit's power, Timothy can walk boldly and radiantly, not thrown off balance by anything. He need not let the difficulties at Ephesus cause him to cower, nor **be ashamed *at all* of the witness of our Lord**. He must confess the Faith boldly and defy persecution. Neither must he be ashamed of Paul, the Lord's **prisoner**, as if being Paul's supporter would make Timothy guilty by association. Rather, let him **suffer hardship** with Paul for the sake of **the Gospel**, suffering **according to *the* power of God**. God will strengthen Timothy by the Spirit he received at ordination. Let young Timothy rely on this power and speak boldly, whatever the cost.

(A note may be added about Timothy's ordination. At that time, a number of people laid their hands on him. St. Paul took the lead in ordaining him and was joined by a number of presbyters as well; compare 1 Tim. 4:14. Paul singles himself out in this account as the chief ordainer because he wants to strengthen the bonds that bind him to Timothy. It is as if he would say to Timothy, "I myself ordained you and empowered you—now don't let me down!")

ॐ ॐ ॐ ॐ ॐ

9   who has saved us and called *us* with a holy
     calling, not according to our works, but according to His own purpose and grace, which was

> given us in Christ Jesus before ages of times,
> 10 but now has been manifested by the appearance of our Savior Christ Jesus, who nullified death and brought to light life and incorruption through the Gospel,
> 11 for which I *myself* was appointed a herald and an apostle and a teacher.

How could Timothy keep silent about this Gospel? God **saved** them once and for all by Christ's Cross and Resurrection (the aorist tense is used, indicating a past and accomplished action). God **called** them in baptism **with a holy calling**. (That is, through saving baptism, He made them *holy*.) This salvation is **not according to our works**, as a reward for accumulated merit. Rather, it is **according to His own purpose** and plan, that of transforming sinners into sons (Rom. 8:28–29) through His own **grace** and unmerited generosity. And the saving plan of God in Christ did not come forth as an accident of history. Rather, it was **given us in Christ Jesus before ages of times**, before the world began (Eph. 1:4). Before the earth was created, God planned such a great salvation and destiny for those who would open their hearts to Him. And this eternal plan is being worked out **now**, in Paul and Timothy's time, being **manifested by the appearance of our Savior Christ Jesus**. **Death** with all its darkness and fear has been **nullified** and abolished by Christ's Cross and Resurrection. Now eternal **life** and the **incorruption** of final resurrection victory have been **brought to light** through **the Gospel**—the very same Gospel of which Paul himself (the pronoun is emphatic) has been **appointed a herald and an apostle and a teacher**. How could Timothy be ashamed of such a glorious message? Or of Paul, its herald? Let Timothy boldly proclaim this Faith to all in Ephesus and to any who will hear!

ॐ ॐ ॐ ॐ ॐ

> 12 For this cause I also suffer these things, but I am not ashamed *at all*, for I know whom I have *put my* faith *in* and I am persuaded that He is

> able to keep *safe* my deposit until that Day.
> 13 Hold to *the* model of healthy words which you
>   heard from me in *the* faith and love that are in
>   Christ Jesus.
> 14 Keep *safe* the good deposit through *the* Holy
>   Spirit dwelling in us.

For this glorious message Paul **suffers these things**. He languishes in prison, not because he is a criminal, but because he identifies himself with this Gospel. He is **not ashamed *at all***, even though slandered as a criminal. He **knows** and experiences the power of the One he has put his **faith** in, and this experience has **persuaded** him that Christ is **able to keep *safe*** Paul's **deposit** until that final **Day**. Paul speaks of his work as a "deposit" (Gr. *paratheke*; compare its use in 1 Tim. 6:20). By this inclusive term Paul refers to the Faith he proclaims, his converts who receive it, and his own life spent in preaching it. He entrusts all his life's work into the Lord's hands, expecting to be rewarded for it. (Thus he speaks of his converts as his "hope" and "joy" and "crown of boasting"; 1 Thess. 2:19.) His impending execution might seem to some to be the undoing of all his work, but Paul knows otherwise. Christ has received his work and will reward him for it on the Last Day.

Timothy too must do the same. He must **hold to *the* model** and paradigm of the apostolic Faith given him by St. Paul, those **healthy** and life-giving **words** that alone can heal the illnesses of the soul. He must do this by walking in truth and holiness, in ***the* faith** (or faithfulness) **and love that are in Christ Jesus** (compare 1 Tim. 1:14). Only by living out the demands of the Gospel can Timothy effectively teach it. Timothy's Gospel is not a dry and academic orthodoxy, but the powerful proclamation coming from a holy life. But Timothy must at all costs preserve the apostolic Tradition. By drawing on the power of ***the* Holy Spirit dwelling** in him, Timothy can **keep *safe* the good deposit** of the Faith. He must proclaim the apostolic Faith and defend it against all distortions, no matter the suffering involved, proclaiming that Faith with zeal through the Holy Spirit as he rekindles His power (compare v. 6).

§IV.   Paul's Situation (1:15–18)

ॐ ॐ ॐ ॐ ॐ

15 You know this, that all the ones in Asia turned away from me, among whom are Phygelus and Hermogenes.

16 The Lord give mercy to the house of Onesiphorus, for he often revived me and was not ashamed *at all* of my chain,

17 but when he was in Rome, he diligently sought me and found *me*—

18 the Lord give to him to find mercy from *the* Lord in that Day—and *in* how many ways he served me in Ephesus you *yourself* know very well.

Having encouraged Timothy from his opening epistolary thanksgiving, Paul then informs him of his present situation. He reminds Timothy of the sad facts he already **knows**—how at Paul's arrest in Ephesus, **all the ones in Asia** (i.e. Asia Minor) **turned away** from him. Far from coming to his help with moral and financial support, they abandoned him, doubtless from fear for their own safety. Particularly disappointing and hurtful was the defection of **Phygelus and Hermogenes**. These two men are otherwise unknown. Perhaps they were two who had previously loudly proclaimed their loyalty and dependability? Perhaps as presbyters of Asia? In any case, Paul singles them out, not so much for blame as to warn Timothy not to depend on them himself. They have proven themselves useless in the hour of crisis, however much they formerly protested their steadfastness. Let Timothy beware of relying on them in the future!

Very different is the example of **Onesiphorus**. He **often revived** Paul and was **not ashamed** *at all* of his **chain** and status as a prisoner. When Onesiphorus **was in Rome**, he **diligently sought** Paul, knocking on doors, making inquiries, and talking to one Roman soldier after another, heedless of the danger. He finally **found** him and "often revived" his spirit, making visit after visit. He was as great a blessing to Paul as the ones in Asia were a disappointment. Timothy should not be surprised at this, for he himself **knows very well** the **many ways** Onesiphorus **served** Paul while both were still **in Ephesus**. (We note in passing how St. Paul chooses to dwell at greater length on the blessings than the disappointments—an example to us as well when we are faced with disappointment and betrayal.)

It would seem, however, that by the time Paul wrote this epistle, Onesiphorus was dead, perhaps from a sudden illness. For it is significant that Paul's first thought and prayer is not for him but rather for his **house** and family. This would be somewhat odd if Onesiphorus were still alive, but quite natural if he had died. And this is confirmed somewhat by Paul's only prayer for him. He does not pray for God to bless his continuing ministry (as we might perhaps expect). Rather, Paul prays that he might be given **mercy from *the* Lord in that Day** of the final Judgment.

This prayer (a short and instinctive utterance, made in the midst of a sentence) is the first instance of prayer for the dead extant in Christian literature. It is an early and apostolic witness to the Church's unbroken practice of commending her dead to God. The Church has always held that the Christian dead are with the Lord, and that it is good nonetheless to commend them to God. Later theology elaborated the rationale behind this, but the practice has always existed.

§V.   Timothy to Persevere in His Work (2:1–26)

ॐ ॐ ॐ ॐ ॐ

2 1   You *yourself* therefore, my child, be empowered in the grace that is in Christ Jesus.

2   And the things which you have heard from me before many witnesses, these commit to faithful men who will be qualified to teach others also.

3   Suffer hardship with *me* as a good soldier of Christ Jesus.

> 4   No one *serving* as soldier gets entangled in the
>   activities of life, that he may please the one who
>   enlisted him.
> 5   And also if anyone competes *as an athlete*, he
>   is not crowned unless he competes lawfully.
> 6   The toiling farmer ought *to be* first to partake
>   of the fruits.
> 7   Think of what I say, for the Lord will give you
>   insight in everything.

Having reflected somewhat on his own situation, Paul turns to Timothy in fatherly tenderness, exhorting him as his **child** to persevere in his work. Timothy himself (the pronoun is emphatic in the Greek) must **be empowered** by the Lord, relying on the **grace** and strength He so freely gives. As an apostle, Timothy must collect the **things which** he **heard** from Paul in his public teaching **before many witnesses** and in turn **commit** these **to faithful men** who are **qualified to teach others also**. This is the original apostolic succession—a succession of teaching. Paul and the first generation of apostles taught the Faith openly to the Church. They entrusted this message and Tradition to others, like Timothy, who would pass it on again to their own generation. Thus the apostolic Tradition is transmitted in unbroken continuity down through the ages.

Since Timothy finds himself surrounded by false teachers in Ephesus, such work of transmission will bring persecution from them. Timothy must faithfully teach the Truth nonetheless and resist all innovations. He must stand up for the pure truth, even though it means he must **suffer hardship** as Paul suffered it; he must endure counterattack and persevere in the battle as would any **good soldier**. Christians live life on the front line, and we must never throw down our arms or flee from the conflict. Rather, we must fight on and not heed the wounds.

To encourage Timothy to persevere, Paul then uses three metaphors, comparing Timothy to a soldier, an athlete, and a farmer. First of all, he reminds Timothy that **no one *serving* as soldier gets entangled in the activities of** civilian **life**. That is, the full-time soldier does not keep a civilian job on the side, working as part-time soldier and part-time restaurateur, for example. His aim is to **please the one who enlisted him**, and so he must devote himself to soldiering full-time.

Also, Paul says, **if anyone competes** *as an athlete* in the Games, he is **not crowned** with the victor's crown **unless he competes lawfully** and according to the rules. That is, he must train full-time. Amateur athletes may train part-time, but those who "compete lawfully" devote themselves to the contest full-time, as professionals, and have no other life. Only thus can they hope to be "crowned" and win the prize.

Finally, Timothy must remember that the **toiling farmer**, the one who works hard, **ought** *to be* **first to partake of the fruits** of his labor and eat from his harvest. Even before the others eat, the farmer who produced the crop has the right to partake first.

What does Paul mean by all these metaphors? Paul, aware that others will read this epistle, does not speak his message forthrightly, but delicately tells Timothy to figure it out for himself. He must **think of what** Paul is saying and of its implications, for **the Lord** will **give** him **insight in everything**. What is this insight that Paul is somewhat reluctant to state plainly? It is that Timothy must resist the temptation to slacken his pace; he must devote himself full-time to the work of teaching and not take up secular employment to support himself. And he must therefore insist on being adequately paid for this work. This is the reason Paul states this in such an indirect way, for he does not want to be accused of mercenary greed. In his own ministry, Paul has always been sensitive to the possibility of this accusation (see 2 Cor. 11:12), and he does not want others to think he is telling Timothy to preach the Gospel for the sake of personal gain. He therefore uses these metaphors, counseling full-time dedication with the right of being rewarded through one's work, and lets Timothy draw the obvious lessons.

ॐ ॐ ॐ ॐ ॐ

8   Remember Jesus Christ, risen from *the* dead, from *the* seed of David, according to my Gospel,

---

> 9 for which I suffer hardship even to bonds as an evil-worker, but the Word of God has not been bound.
>
> 10 Therefore I endure all things because of the chosen ones, that they also may attain salvation in Christ Jesus with *its* eternal glory.
>
> 11 Faithful *is* the word: for
> If we co-died with Him, we will also co-live with Him;
>
> 12 If we endure, we will also co-reign with Him;
> If we deny, that One also will deny us;
>
> 13 If we are faithless, that One remains faithful, for He is not able to deny Himself.

Timothy must commit himself to the proclamation of the historic and apostolic Gospel, shunning innovation. At all times, he is to **remember Jesus Christ** as preached by the apostles—not the gnostic version of Jesus, a Jesus without a tangible physical body, a Jesus who only seems to be real, a Jesus who never really died. Rather, Timothy must proclaim the Jesus Christ who truly died and who is **risen from *the* dead**, the One who has true physical existence, the Jesus Christ who was **from *the* seed of David** and descended from an historic lineage, the One who is **according to** Paul's **Gospel**, not the pseudo-gospel of the heretics.

It is for this Gospel that Paul **suffers hardship** and persecution, **even to** the point of **bonds** and imprisonment as if he were **an evil-worker** and criminal. Being true to the Gospel inevitably means enduring difficulties, but Timothy must not flinch, no matter what. Though the preacher may be in bonds, **the Word of God** preached **has not been bound**. It remains forever free and will do its work in the faithful long after the preacher is gone. Therefore the preacher (like Paul) must **endure all things because of the chosen ones**, the new converts who through faith become God's chosen people. Regardless of what the preacher may have to suffer, he must remain steadfast and not apostatize or give up, lest his converts see this and be tempted to give up as well. He must endure all things as an example of perseverance to these converts, so that **they also may** finally **attain salvation in Christ Jesus** on the Last Day with its promise of **eternal glory**. Glory and everlasting reward await them all!—but only if they hold fast their original Faith.

St. Paul here gives the **faithful** and reliable **word** of the Church, probably quoting from a church hymn. He adds his own comment at the end, **for He is not able to deny Himself**. The hymn is arranged in a series of three parallelisms, which together celebrate the need for and reward of endurance.

The hymn begins by promising eternal life as the reward for faithfulness: **if we co-died with Him** (Gr. *sunapothnesko*) in baptism and through this sacrament of faith have shared His death on the Cross (Rom. 6:3–8), **we will also co-live with Him** (Gr. *suzao*) and share His eternal resurrection life. **If we endure** and persevere in the midst of suffering, then (and only then) **we will also co-reign with Him** (Gr. *sumbasileuo*), sharing His glory in the age to come. (The aspect of sharing these realities by virtue of our union with Christ, of our sharing His own experiences of death, new life, and kingly authority, is expressed in Greek by the *su-* prefix of the verbs used, rendered in English as "co-.")

But this life and glory are not automatic. They presuppose our continued faithfulness to the original message. For **if we deny** the Faith and disown our Master, **that One also will deny us** at the Judgment. If we fall away from Christ, if we **are faithless** and deny our Master through apostasy or heresy, **that One remains faithful** to His Word and will disown us in turn at the end, "for He is not able to deny Himself" or retract His Word. He promised that He would confess those who confessed Him and deny those who denied Him (Matt. 10:32–33), and He will prove Himself true to that promise. Let all His people hearken and learn from this church hymn!

ॐ ॐ ॐ ॐ ॐ

14 Remind them of these things, and testify before God that they may not word-quarrel, which is useful for nothing, but *leads* to the destruction of the hearers.

> 15 Be diligent to present yourself to God *as one* approved, an unashamed workman, rightly-defining the Word of Truth.
>
> 16 But stand-back from profane empty-talk, for it will advance to further impiety,
>
> 17 and their word will have a spread *effect* like gangrene.

Timothy must **remind** his hearers in Ephesus of **these things** (i.e. the instructions outlined in vv. 8–13) and solemnly **testify before God**, who hears all their words, that they are **not** to **word-quarrel**. The verb rendered "word-quarrel" is the Greek *logomacheo*, which is cognate with the noun *logomachia*, used in 1 Tim. 6:4 and also rendered "word-quarrel." The verb means to fight over mere words, to nitpick and argue over verbal trifles. This is what the would-be teachers of the Law do (see 1 Tim. 1:6–7). They offer wild and improbable interpretations of every word in the Law, indulging in myths and allegories. All this is nothing other than **profane empty-talk**, sacrilegious babbling, philosophical room-noise (compare 1 Tim. 6:20). Timothy must **stand-back** from these things and avoid entering into disputes. For such disputes are not useful for spiritual growth, nor do they lead to increased piety in the hearers. On the contrary, they are **useful for nothing** and lead only to **the destruction of the hearers**, to spiritual catastrophe. (The word translated "destruction" is the Gr. *katastrophe*, used also in Gen. 19:29 LXX to describe the overthrow of Sodom and Gomorrah.) Timothy must avoid such things altogether, for those who indulge in such dubious studies advance **to further impiety**, not to further piety. The **word** of the false teachers has a **spread** *effect* like **gangrene**; it eats up their spiritual life as spreading sores eat up flesh and leaves them to a painful death.

Timothy's teaching must be otherwise. He must **be diligent** and hasten to work hard at preaching, careful to **present** himself **to God** *as one* **approved**. When God inspects his teaching ministry on the Last Day, let Him find it blameless, not shoddy and full of self-deluded nonsense like that of the false teachers. Let Timothy

117

prove himself **an unashamed workman**, one who can proudly present to God his work of preaching, confident that he has preserved the Gospel in its purity. Let him **rightly-define the Word of Truth**, the Christian Gospel.

The word translated here as "rightly-define" is the Greek *orthotomeo*. (The present translation is borrowed from the OCA liturgical translation of the term; see the anaphora, where the bishops are said to "rightly define the Word of [God's] Truth.") The word literally means "to rightly cut." It is used in Prov. 3:6; 11:5 LXX with the meaning "to cut a correct path or choose the right way [e.g. through a forest]"; it is translated "to rightly direct" or "to trace out." By using this verb here, Paul exhorts Timothy to choose the correct interpretation of Scripture, heading straight for God's truth, avoiding the false paths and dead-ends of the would-be teachers. In other words, he must indeed "rightly-define" the Truth of the Gospel, teaching it with fidelity to the apostolic Tradition and rejecting the new paths of the heretics.

ॐ ॐ ॐ ॐ ॐ

17 Among them are Hymenaeus and Philetus,
18 who have missed *the mark* concerning the Truth, saying that the resurrection has already occurred, and thus they are overturning the faith of some.
19 Nevertheless the solid foundation of God has stood *firm*, having this seal: "The Lord knows the ones who are His," and "Let everyone who names the Name of *the* Lord depart from unrighteousness."

As examples of such heresy and of how it can quickly and lethally spread, St. Paul mentions **Hymenaeus and Philetus**. This Hymenaeus is probably the same as the one mentioned in 1 Tim.

1:20, where he is said to have been excommunicated along with an otherwise unknown Alexander. Nothing more is known of Philetus. He seems to have been a partner with Hymenaeus in this particular heresy. The nature of this heresy pertained to the final **resurrection** of the flesh. Pagan thought found the resurrection of the body both absurd and repugnant (see Acts 17:32). It would seem that Hymenaeus and Philetus found it so as well and tried to spiritualize it away, perhaps equating it with our spiritual death and resurrection in Holy Baptism (see Rom. 6:3f), saying that it had **already occurred** and was not therefore to occur again in any physical sense. The only resurrection, they said, was the spiritual resurrection of baptism; it would be unthinkable to suggest that God would raise up our bodies again after we had been liberated from them! In saying this, they have **missed *the mark* concerning the Truth** of the Faith (compare 1 Tim. 6:6, 21). Their teaching was catching on, and they were even then **overturning the faith of some**. Timothy must deal with this threat and refute their teaching—and remember what harm such "profane empty-talk" (v. 16) can do.

Timothy should not be surprised at such challenges nor disheartened by them. God has built the Church on a **solid foundation**. It **has stood *firm*** and will continue to stand firm, surviving all heretical assaults against it. Just as the architect puts an inscription on his building, so God also put his **seal** upon the Church.

The words of this seal may be taken from another hymn of the Church, perhaps produced as a prophetic utterance by one of the prophets (compare 1 Tim. 4:1, 14). They indicate that **the Lord** God **knows** and protects those **who are His** own (see Ps. 1:6), defending them from all assaults. And they must show that they are truly His own by their righteousness and piety. **Everyone who names the Name of *the* Lord** in baptism and who claims to be His follower must show he is His by **departing from unrighteousness**. Only by their holy and pious lives can they claim His divine protection and be acknowledged by Him as His own.

> ॐ ॐ ॐ ॐ ॐ
>
> 20 Now in a great house there are not only golden and silver vessels, but also wooden and earthen *ones*, and some for honor, but others for dishonor.
>
> 21 Therefore if anyone cleanses himself from these things, he will be a vessel for honor, having been sanctified, useful to the Master, prepared for every good work.

It is the same as in any **great house**: many **vessels** are to be found in it, some for honorable use (such as drinking vessels, the **golden and silver** ones) and some for dishonorable use (such as containers for garbage, the **wooden and earthen** ones). In the same way, there are many kinds of people in the great household of God, the Church: some who walk in righteousness and are headed **for honor**, and some who walk in unrighteousness and are headed **for dishonor**.

Yet here there is no fatalism or arbitrary predestination. **Anyone** may be saved and destined for honor if he so wills. Let him only **cleanse himself from these things** (i.e. from the sins characterizing the unrighteous who are headed for dishonor and damnation) and **he will be a vessel for honor**. He will have been **sanctified**, having separated himself from the unrighteous ways of the impious world; he will then be **useful to the Master** of the house and **prepared for every good work** to which He might call him. The false teachers have rejected the claims of conscience (see 1 Tim. 1:19–20). They are useless to the Christ they claim to serve and cannot be used by Him for any good work (such as leading people to holiness through their teaching). If anyone steers clear of them and their ways, such a person can be useful indeed to the Lord.

> ॐ ॐ ॐ ॐ ॐ
>
> 22 Now flee from youthful lusts and pursue righteousness, faith, love, peace, with the ones who call on the Lord from a clean heart.
>
> 23 But reject foolish and uneducated debates,

> knowing that they beget quarrels.
>
> 24 And the Lord's slave must not quarrel, but be gentle to all, *able to* teach, forbearing,
>
> 25 with meekness disciplining the opposing ones, if perhaps God may give them repentance *leading* to the real-knowledge of the Truth,
>
> 26 and they may sober up and *escape* from the snare of the devil, having been caught by him to *do* that one's will.

Timothy, as someone who aspires to be useful to the Master, must himself **flee from youthful lusts** and **pursue righteousness**. That is, he must run *away* from sin and *toward* holiness. In particular, he must pursue **faith** and trustworthiness in all his relationships, both to God and to men. He must show **love** to all, which is seen not in any fleeting feeling of warmth, but in a determination to serve. He must run after **peace**, attaining an inner equilibrium that outer circumstances cannot shake. And this successful flight from youthful lusts and attainment of the opposite virtues can take place only as Timothy pursues and remains in the company of **the ones who call on the Lord from a clean heart**. The human personality is dynamic, not static; and the heart is affected by those around it. If we continually spend time with those who delight in worldly values, it will inevitably affect us too. Obviously Paul does not forbid all social interaction with non-Christians. But he says that Timothy must seek his close friends among the saints.

But in spending time with the Christians, Timothy must take care not to spend that time arguing. In fact, he must positively refuse to join in the arguments when they occur. He must **reject foolish and uneducated debates**. Such "discussions" (as the combatants would call them) do not result in holiness and harmony. All they are good for is to produce and **beget quarrels** and ill-feeling. And **the Lord's slave** (as Timothy aspires to be) **must not quarrel**. That is, the slave must not be concerned about his own will (which is the source of all quarreling) but only about doing the Master's will.

Instead of being contentious, Timothy has been called by God to win over **the opposing ones** who resist the Church's teaching. To do this, he must be **gentle to all** (Gr. *epios*; compare its use in 1 Thess. 2:7, where it describes a nursing mother cherishing her children). He must be *able to* **teach**, having a teacher's heart. He must be **forbearing** (Gr. *anexikakos*, lit. "putting up with wickedness"), being patient without resentment when wronged. He must **discipline** and teach "the opposing ones," but **with meekness**, not with arrogance or a sense of superiority, lest he alienate those he hopes to win. The word translated "discipline" is the Greek *paideuo*. It is cognate with *paideia*, or "upbringing" (compare its use in Eph. 6:4, where Paul uses it to describe the upbringing in which fathers are to nourish their children). Timothy must not lecture his opponents, but correct and educate them with all the patience fathers should have for their own children.

Timothy must use this godly polemic and correction not simply to prove himself right, but in the hope that **perhaps God may give them repentance *leading* to the real-knowledge** and recognition (Gr. *epignosis*) **of the Truth**. Timothy should have compassion for those who resist the Church's teaching, for they have been taken in **the snare of the devil** and have lost their spiritual senses; they have been **caught by him to *do* that one's will**. The word rendered "caught" (Gr. *zogreo*) has the sense of being captured alive. Such captives are no longer free or able to do their own will, but have been caught and caged by the devil and are entirely enslaved. As such, they deserve compassion, not anger. Perhaps through Timothy's teaching God will give them another opportunity for repentance, and they will **sober up** and come to their senses again (Gr. *ananepho*; compare *nepho*, "to be sober"). Meanwhile, Timothy must deal with them as patiently as he can, hoping and praying for God's mercy to enlighten them.

§VI.   The Challenge of Evil Men (3:1–17)

ॐ ॐ ॐ ॐ ॐ

3 1   But know this, that in *the* last days, dangerous times will come.

> 2 For men will be self-lovers, money-lovers,
>   boastful, arrogant, revilers, unobedient to
>   parents, ungrateful, unholy,
> 3 unloving, unreconcilable, slanderers, uncon-
>   trolled, untamed, not lovers-of-good,
> 4 traitors, reckless, conceited, pleasure-lovers
>   rather than God-lovers;
> 5 having a form of piety, though they have denied
>   its power; and turn away from these ones.

St. Paul warns his young colleague of the perils and challenges to come. Timothy must pursue righteousness (2:22), but he must do so in a world increasingly hostile to it. He must **know this** for certain and have no doubts that his task will be long and arduous. The **last days** (that is, the eschatological time in which they were living; see 1 Cor. 7:31; 10:11; 1 John 2:18) are **dangerous times** and can only get more dangerous. A flood of evil is about to **come** and Timothy must be ready.

The word translated "dangerous" (Gr. *chalepos*) means "hard to bear." Matthew uses it in Matt. 8:28 to describe the Gadarene demoniacs; there it is translated "violent." The days about to break upon Timothy will be difficult to endure and filled with peril.

This peril will come from the hearts of men and from the opposition they will mount. **Men will be self-lovers** (Gr. *philautos*) and **money-lovers** (Gr. *philarguros*), interested only in feeding their own egos and advancing their own plans, and greedy for money as the way of accomplishing this. They will be **boastful** braggarts (Gr. *alazon*), **arrogant** showoffs (Gr. *uperephanos*), and **revilers** Gr. *blasphemos*) who delight to insult others and put them down to make themselves look important.

Paul then uses a series of five words, all beginning with the so-called "alpha-privative"—the "a-" prefix that acts like a negative, like our English prefix "un-." Paul fires off these words like so many cracks of a whip, the initial "a" sound making for greater emphasis. He declares that men will be *goneusin apatheis, acharistoi, anosioi, astorgoi, aspondoi*. That is, **unobedient to parents, ungrateful, unholy, unloving, unreconcilable**. (The "un-" prefix is retained here even at the cost of poor English, to convey the feel of the repeated alpha-privative.) Paul then says that men will be **slanderers** (Gr. *diaboloi*, lit. "devils," that is, malicious gossips), and then sets in with another series of alpha-privatives. Men will be *akrteis, anemeroi, aphilagathoi*. That is, **uncontrolled, untamed, not lovers-of-good**.

It is an astonishing catalogue of denunciation and one worth a bit of verbal unpacking. Paul says that men will be "unobedient to parents," caring nothing for the first and most basic of all human duties. They will be "ungrateful" to anyone, taking advantage of friends without scruple. They will be "unholy," trampling down all the demands of piety and decency. They will be "unloving" (Gr. *astorgoi*), lacking in *storge* or natural affection, able to coldly practice abortion and infanticide. They will be "unreconcilable" (Gr. *aspondos*, lit. "without treaty or truce"), refusing to forgive or make peace.

In addition, they will be "uncontrolled" (Gr. *akrateis*, lit. "without strength"), utterly unable to govern their desires; they will be "untamed" (Gr. *anemeroi*), brutal and savage, devoid of sympathy for the suffering; they will be "not lovers-of-good" (Gr. *aphilagathoi*), despising goodness as if it were mere weakness, delighting only in power. (Though this last is an alpha-privative as well, it resists being translated with the English prefix "un-" even more than the others.)

More than that, men will be **traitors** (Gr. *prodotes*, the same word used in Luke 6:16 to describe Judas Iscariot), betraying one another with serene conscience. They will be **reckless** (Gr. *propetes*, lit., "falling forward") and rash, swept on by passion, never stopping to weigh the consequences of their actions. They will be **conceited** (Gr. *tuphoo*) and blinded by arrogance. They will be **pleasure-lovers** (Gr. *philedonos*) rather than **God-lovers** (Gr. *philotheos*), worshipping pleasure as the ultimate aim and goal in life.

These men **have a form of piety** and will hold to the appearance of religion, delighting in religious controversy and promoting themselves as the wisest of teachers. Nonetheless, they **have denied**

its power, rejecting the call of conscience and caring nothing for a transformed life. Timothy must **turn away from these ones** and have nothing to do with them.

☙ ☙ ☙ ☙ ☙

6   For among them are those who enter into houses and capture weak-women heaped-up with sins, led by various desires,

7   always learning and never able to come to the real-knowledge of the Truth.

8   And in the way that Jannes and Jambres withstood Moses, thus also these withstand the Truth, men of damaged mind, unapproved concerning the Faith.

9   But they will not advance *any* further, for their folly will be plain to all, as also the *folly* of those came to be.

It will be a hard battle for Timothy, as he strives to counteract the work of these religious charlatans. For these false teachers will have some measure of success. They will **enter into houses**, worming their way in with their grandiose promises of enlightenment, and **capture weak-women**.

The word translated "weak-women" is the Greek *gunaikarion*, the diminutive for "woman." It literally means "little woman" but was used with a negative connotation, in the sense of "silly little woman" or "weak-willed woman." These women are **heaped-up with sins** and vulnerable to anyone who promises relief; they are **led** and lured **by various desires**, which dominate them; they are **always learning** and following the latest fad, but are **never able to come to the real-knowledge** and reognition **of the Truth**. These formthe main targets and victims of the false teachers and their main sponsors. That such women sing their praises is no commendation!

But though they might enjoy success for a time, Timothy need not fear. **Jannes and Jambres withstood Moses** too, but the Truth

125

ultimately prevailed and they were seen for what they were. It will be **thus also** with **these** false teachers who now **withstand the Truth** of the Gospel—these **men of damaged** and corrupted **mind** who are incapable of recognizing the Truth, who are **unapproved concerning the Faith**, who are found to be useless for the task of teaching the Gospel.

Paul refers here to the contest of the Egyptian magicians with Moses in Ex. 7:11f. (The Jewish Targum, or translation into Aramaic, gives these men the names Jannes and Jambres, and Paul uses these names for ease of identification, regardless of questions of historicity.) The men were Moses' rivals as he strove to convince Pharaoh of his divine authority, even as the false teachers are Timothy's rivals as he strives to win the hearts of men for the Gospel. And just as Jannes and Jambres could not keep up with the power of Moses (since Moses had the true God on his side and Jannes and Jambres were counterfeits), so also Timothy's rivals will eventually be shown up for the counterfeits they are. Though Timothy's competition may make some progress, they will reach a place where **they will not advance *any* further, for their folly will be plain to all**. It is this way throughout history: heretical fads may spring up and prosper for a time, but when the fad passes, all will see the heresy for the nonsense it is. Timothy must labor on, confident of the final victory of his cause.

ॐ ॐ ॐ ॐ ॐ

10 But you *yourself* have followed along with my teaching, conduct, purpose, faith, patience, love, perseverance,

11 persecutions, sufferings, what happened to me in Antioch, in Iconium, in Lystra, what persecutions I endured, out of them all the Lord rescued me!

12 And indeed, all the ones desiring to live piously in Christ Jesus will be persecuted.

Regardless of the challenge of evil men, therefore, Timothy must stay the course. Paul exhorts his protégé to follow in his footsteps and learn from his life. He points to him as one who has had this privileged education (we can almost see Paul's finger directed at his young friend; the **you** is emphatic in the Greek) and sets out before him all of his life's lessons. Timothy has **followed along**, carefully observing Paul as a disciple watching his mentor. He heard his **teaching** which he gave in public to the churches and how it stressed the necessity of a holy life (unlike these false teachers). He observed Paul's **conduct** and blameless way of life and how he always followed the dictates of conscience, putting others before himself. He saw his **purpose** and resolution, how he never swerved from fulfilling his God-given mission, regardless of the cost. He saw his **faith** and reliability and how he always kept his word; his **patience** and how he endured slander without becoming bitter; his **love** for all and how he freely gave his heart to his converts; his **perseverance** and how he bravely bore up under sufferings, refusing to lose heart.

More than that, when with him, Timothy observed also Paul's **persecutions** and **sufferings**, such as hunger, thirst, and sleeplessness (2 Cor. 11:27). He knows what Paul experienced **in Antioch** (i.e. Pisidian Antioch) and how he was rejected by the Jews there (Acts 13:14f). He remembers what happened to Paul **in Iconium**, where an attempt was made to rough Paul up and stone him so that he had to flee for his life (Acts 14:1f). He remembers what befell Paul **in Lystra** and how he was actually stoned, hurt so badly he was left for dead (Acts 14:8f). Timothy can remember all these experiences, as well as the lesson Paul draws from them: that **out of them all the Lord rescued** him. And so, Paul says, the Lord will rescue Timothy too in his own hour of trial. For Timothy will indeed suffer as Paul has, count on it! And not he only, but **all the ones desiring to live piously in Christ Jesus will be persecuted**, so Timothy should prepare himself now to endure this. But Timothy need not fear, for the Lord will rescue him too.

ॐ ॐ ॐ ॐ ॐ

13 But evil men and swindlers will advance to the worst, deceiving and being deceived.

---

14 You *yourself*, however, remain in the things you learned and put your faith in, knowing from whom you learned *them*;

15 and that from infancy you have known the sacred Writings which are able to make you wise for salvation through faith in Christ Jesus.

16 All Scripture *is* God-breathed and profitable for teaching, for reproof, for correction, for discipline in righteousness,

17 that the man of God may be proficient, equipped for every good work.

Timothy need not, therefore, worry about the opposition of evil men. They will always be there, all the **evil men and swindlers**, and they will **advance to the worst**, continuing their wretched journey downward. They are **being deceived** themselves, and they will naturally go on **deceiving** others, spreading the error in which they themselves are taken.

The word translated here "swindlers" (Gr. *goes*) originally meant "a wailer" and then came to mean "a sorcerer," probably because their sorcerous spells were uttered with a wailing sound. The word finally came to mean a swindler, a con-man, an imposter, and it bears this meaning here. Just as Jannes and Jambres were counterfeit sorcerers, so Timothy's evil rivals are counterfeits too—mere spiritual swindlers, running a shell-game with their words. Timothy should just leave them alone, for he is on a different path. He himself (the pronoun is again emphatic) must **remain in the things** he **learned** and has **put** his **faith in, knowing from whom** he **learned** them. That is, he has learned from Paul and his life's lessons that he is on the right course; let him stay that course. Long-term perseverance is the key. He must not let the fleeting success of his rivals cause him to change his message to be more like theirs in the hope of gaining more success himself. The example of Paul should steady him in times of temptation.

More than that, as well as knowing the example of Paul's life, he has **known the sacred Writings** of the Old Testament Scripture

from infancy. Paul's message is nothing other than the proclamation that these Writings are now being fulfilled.

The term *sacred Writings* (Gr. *iera grammata*, lit. the "ieratic letters") refers to the sacred Scrolls of the Law that Timothy has seen in synagogues ever since he can remember. Paul declares to him that these Scriptures, the Jewish Law, are **able to make** him **wise for salvation through faith in Christ Jesus**. That is, the Jewish faith leads to the Christian Faith, and the hope of the Law finds its fulfillment in the Gospel. The goal of all Timothy's Jewish upbringing is to become wise and to know God, to experience the salvation that is only available through faith in Christ Jesus. Let Timothy be true to what he has known all his life!

Indeed, Paul continues, in Christ, **all Scripture *is* God-breathed and profitable for teaching, for reproof, for correction, for discipline in righteousness**. The Scripture (by which Paul means only the Old Testament; the New Testament as a body had not yet been fully written and collected) is "profitable" to him even now as a Christian and can aid him in his work. Though given to the Jews in ancient time, Scripture actually finds its fulfillment in Christ. That is because the Jewish Scriptures are not merely literary examples of Hebrew culture, but are also "God-breathed" (Gr. *theopneustos*), the work of the Spirit of God, who transcends all times and cultures. (The word for "Spirit" and "breath" is the same in Greek—*pneuma*, as it is also in Hebrew—*ruach*.) Though the Scriptures are the works of men, God was also involved in their creation by His Spirit, so that Hebrew Scripture has a prophetic element.

Timothy, aware that his ancestral Writings speak of his present Christian Faith, can use them in his own teaching ministry. They are useful "for reproof" (Gr. *elegmos*; compare its use in Num. 5:18 LXX) and exposing the sins of those in the Church. They are for "correction" and restoring the sinner, bringing him to an upright position (the literal meaning of the Gr. *epanorthosis*). They are profitable for "discipline" and spiritual upbringing as the children of God (Gr. *paideia*; compare its use to describe the training of children in Eph. 6:4).

With the Scriptures, Timothy as a **man of God** is **proficient** and fully qualified to fulfill his work. He is **equipped for every good work**. He does not need to supplement the Scriptures and Faith of the Church with further gnostic fantasies. The false teachers might allow that the Scriptures are an acceptable place to start one's faith journey, but they assert the Scriptures need to be supplemented with their own gnostic concepts and teaching for one to reach maturity. Paul assures Timothy that the Scriptures, interpreted by the apostolic Tradition, are all he needs.

§VII. Timothy to Preach Urgently (4:1–8)

4 1   I testify before God and Christ Jesus, who is about to judge *the* living and *the* dead, and by His appearance and His Kingdom:

2   herald the Word; stand ready in season *and* out of season; expose, rebuke, exhort, with all patience and teaching.

3   For the time will be when they will not bear with healthy teaching, but according to their own desires will accumulate teachers for themselves to tickle the ear,

4   and will turn away the ear from the Truth, and will turn aside to myths.

Paul begins his final written encouragement for Timothy, summoning all the moral authority he can as he solemnly **testifies before God and Christ Jesus**. Through this magnificent and weighty charge, Paul impresses on his young colleague the importance and urgency of this task. He describes Christ Jesus as **about to** (Gr. *mellontos*) **judge *the* living and *the* dead**, not because the Second Coming is chronologically near but because Christ stands ready to judge even now. God and Christ Jesus see and hear all, and no deeds can be done—or duties omitted!—without Their knowledge. Paul also adjures Timothy by Christ's **appearance and**

His Kingdom, that is, by His Second Coming and the new age it will bring. When the Lord returns, judgment will come with its rewards and censures; Timothy must remember this and fulfill his charge.

And this is his charge: he must **herald the Word** of the Gospel. The word rendered "herald" (Gr. *kerusso*) means to proclaim like a herald and is cognate with the noun *kerux*, "a herald." That is, Timothy is to preach the Gospel with all the authority of one bringing the proclamation of a King, and he must **stand ready** to do this **in season *and* out of season**, all the time, regardless of the perceived receptivity of his audience. In his ministry, he must always be on duty, always standing by and prepared to make known the Good News. He must **expose, rebuke,** and **exhort**, exposing error, confronting the sinners, encouraging all to come to righteousness and truth. And he must do this **with all patience and teaching**. As he corrects their errors, he must never lose patience and must carefully instruct them in the correct way. Scolding them for going the wrong way is not enough; he must show them the right path.

This is urgent work, and he must not wait until he thinks they want to learn. For the days will soon come **when they will not bear with** and put up with **healthy teaching** at all. Rather, **according to their own desires** and passions, they will **accumulate teachers for themselves to tickle the ear**. That is, they will go through teacher after teacher, choosing each one on the basis that he will tell them only what they want to hear. They will **turn away the ear** from hearing **the Truth**, for they only want to be tickled and pleasured and entertained, and will **turn aside** to the **myths** that their false teachers provide (compare 1 Tim. 1:4). There will be no place for Timothy's teaching then! He must therefore do all he can now to put his message before them.

---

৯৮ ৯৮ ৯৮ ৯৮ ৯৮

5 But you *yourself,* be sober in all things, suffer hardship, do *the* work of an evangelist, fulfill your ministry.

6 For I *myself* am already being poured-out-as-

> a-drink-offering, and the time of my release
> stands ready.
> 7 I have *striven in* contest the good contest,
>   I have finished the course, I have kept the
>   Faith;
> 8 henceforth there is laid up for me the crown
>   of righteousness which the Lord, the righteous
>   Judge, will render to me in that Day; and not
>   only to me, but also to all the ones who have
>   loved His appearance.

Timothy himself (the emphatic pronoun is used) must **be sober in all things**, in all circumstances. The word translated "be sober" (Gr. *nepho*) denotes not simply physical sobriety and the avoidance of drunkenness, but also an inner vigilance of spirit. Persecution may come, but he must not shrink from it; he must **suffer hardship** and continue to **do *the* work of an evangelist** and **fulfill** his **ministry**. An "evangelist" (Gr. *euaggelistes*) was one who traveled and preached the Gospel (Gr. *euaggelion*) to the unconverted; it is used of Philip in Acts 21:8 (compare Philip's work in Acts 8:5f). Though not traveling to other cities, Timothy is still to do this work also, striving to reach the unconverted where he lives in Ephesus.

Regarding Paul himself, his work of ministry is done. (The emphatic pronoun is used here too, in parallel with v. 5, as if to say, "This is what *you* must do; as for *me*, I am finished doing.") He is **already being poured-out-as-a-drink-offering**. The verb used is the Greek *spendo* (used also in Phil. 2:17), which denotes the drink-offering or libation poured out on a sacrifice just before it is burned (see Lev. 23:13). Paul considers his blood shed in martyrdom as a drink-offering poured on the sacrifice of his convert's faith, and as his self-offering to God. This has *already* begun, since he is facing the sentence of death and **the time** of his **release stands ready**. Paul does not regard death as a dark tragedy to be feared, but as his "release" (Gr. *analusis*) from this earth and his return to his Lord (compare Phil. 1:23, with its cognate verb *analuo*).

He faces this return with confidence, knowing he has *striven in*

contest the good contest, finished the course, and **kept the Faith**.
In the future, there is **laid up** for him a winner's **crown of righteousness**. The sustained metaphor used is from the athletic games. (The
phrase rendered "striven in contest the good contest"—*ton kalon
agona egonismai*—could be translated "fought the good fight," but
Paul seems to use the verb *agonizomai* as an echo of the Games; see
1 Cor. 9:25.) St. Paul here compares himself to a runner. He has
given his all in the race of Faith and is about to cross the finish-line.
Now the victor's crown awaits him, even as winners in the Games
were awarded a wreath of leaves (1 Cor. 9:25). And this reward of
eternal glory is not for Paul only, but for **all the ones who have
loved** Christ's **appearance** in humility on earth, and who thus walk
in the way of righteousness. If Timothy will persevere in his work,
the Lord Jesus, as **the righteous Judge**, will see his perseverance and
render to him that same crown as well!

§VIII. Final Personal Admonitions (4:9–21)

ॐ ॐ ॐ ॐ ॐ

9   Be diligent to come to me soon;
10 for Demas, having loved this present age,
has left me behind and gone to Thessalonica;
Crescens to Galatia; Titus to Dalmatia.
11 Luke alone is with me. Take Mark and bring
him with you, for he is useful to me for service.
12 But Tychicus I have sent to Ephesus.
13 When you come, bring the cloak which I left
with Carpus in Troas, and the books, especially
the parchments.

St. Paul then leaves final personal instructions. With heart-
rending pathos, as one lonely for his friend, he begs Timothy to
be diligent and make every effort to **come to** him **soon**. (Indeed,
so greatly does he want his friend's company that he returns to the
request again in v. 21, begging him to "come before winter," when
stormy sea conditions will make the journey impossible.) And he

tells him why: Most everyone has gone and he is lonely for Christian company. **Demas** (mentioned in Col. 4:14 and Philemon 24 as his "co-worker") has **loved this present age** and apostatized from the Faith. Staying with the condemned Paul was too dangerous for him; he **left behind** his former co-worker and returned to the world.

Others, though not loving the world and leaving the Faith, have also gone away on other errands: **Crescens** (not mentioned elsewhere) has gone **to Galatia** in Asia Minor, and **Titus** (who had finished his work in Crete by this time) has gone on **to Dalmatia**, across the Adriatic Sea. **Luke alone** is with him (possibly staying in his capacity as physician to attend to the apostle in his failing health?). Paul therefore pines for Timothy's company. When he comes, he is to **take Mark** (perhaps en route to Rome? or was Mark then in Ephesus?) and **bring *him*** with him, for he is **useful** to Paul **for service**. We note that Paul once quarreled over Mark, considering him quite useless for service (Acts 15:36–40), but this quarrel has long since been healed.

Paul mentions that he has **sent** his old comrade **Tychicus** on **to Ephesus**, where Timothy is. Though this "sent" could be an epistolary aorist (i.e. "I am now sending him") so that Tychicus is the bearer of the epistle, I suggest that it refers to a prior sending, for otherwise it would state the obvious. Obviously Tychicus has been sent to Ephesus, for there he is standing in front of Timothy! It seems more likely that Paul is not stating the obvious, but is telling Timothy that Tychicus has already been sent to Ephesus (perhaps by a more circuitous route than the bearer of the epistle) and is expected to arrive there later. Paul's reason for mentioning this is that the Ephesian church should prepare themselves to welcome Tychicus as Timothy's replacement when he arrives there.

Paul adds a note of personal instruction. When Timothy comes, he should stop **in Troas** to pick up **the cloak** that Paul left there **with Carpus**. The word translated "cloak" (Gr. *phailone;* compare the contemporary priestly vestment, the *phelon*) referred to a large garment like a poncho, probably made out of Cilician goats' hair. It was very warm and Paul had left it with Carpus previously, probably during the warm summer weather. Now that he is facing the cold damp of a Roman prison in winter, he needs his warm cloak again.

He also wants **the books** or scrolls (Gr. *ta biblia*) and **especially the parchments**. What were these books and parchments? It is impossible to say with certainty, but I would suggest the books were copies of the Scriptures, written on the usual papyrus, perhaps volumes of the prophets. As Paul awaited execution, reading them would comfort him as he saw his own work mirrored in those ancient words (compare Acts 13:47). Paul was especially anxious to have the parchments of vellum (or animal skin), which were more precious and expensive than papyrus scrolls. These perhaps were also copies of the Scriptures, and more precious to him since they were (perhaps) the gift of his parents to him from his childhood. That is, these parchments had a sentimental value as well, and the great apostle wanted to have them with him as he faced his end.

ॐ ॐ ॐ ॐ ॐ

14 Alexander the coppersmith demonstrated many wicked things against me; the Lord will render to him according to his works.

15 Guard against him yourself also, for he greatly withstood our words.

16 At my first defense no one *stood* beside me, but all left me behind; may it not be reckoned to them.

17 But the Lord stood with me and empowered me, that through me the heralding might be fulfilled and all the Gentiles might hear; and I was rescued out of the lion's mouth.

18 The Lord will rescue me from every evil work and will save me to His heavenly Kingdom; to whom be glory to the ages of the ages. Amen.

Paul then turns to thoughts of his own end. He remembers both the betrayals of the past and how God stood with him despite it all. In particular he warns Timothy against **Alexander**, identified

as **the coppersmith** to distinguish him from the Alexander of
1 Tim. 1:20. He **demonstrated many wicked things against** Paul.
The word rendered "demonstrated" (Gr. *endeiknumi*) is often used
of an informer laying charges against someone. Perhaps Alexander
turned against Paul at his arrest and vigorously accused him to save
his own skin? Paul does not dwell on it or allow himself to become
bitter. He simply says that **the Lord will render to him according to his works**. God will judge him, and Paul need not concern
himself with the matter further. Here is an example in dealing with
those who betray us! We must not fixate on the offense when we are
hurt, but leave all to God. But also, let us not be naive! Paul warns
Timothy to **guard against him** also and not rely on him. For he
greatly withstood and opposed the apostolic **words** and message.
The threat he poses should not be minimized, for he will doubtless
seek to harm Timothy too.

Alexander's opposition is not the only disappointment. At Paul's
first defense (or preliminary hearing), **no one** *stood* **beside** him and
supported him, but **all left** him **behind** and deserted him. Showing public support for Paul was too dangerous, and the Christian
community in Rome thought it best to keep well away from the
notorious prisoner. Once again, St. Paul does not allow himself to
become embittered. In the spirit of his Master, he simply says, **may
it not be reckoned to them** (compare Luke 23:34). (We note in
passing how Saul the persecutor now takes the place of one he once
persecuted and shares his forgiving spirit; see Acts 7:60.)

For though men might disappoint us, **the Lord** never will.
He **stood with** Paul at that defense when all others had fled and
empowered him with His Spirit, giving him boldness to declare
the Gospel. Paul, as he had long since prayed (see Eph. 6:19), used
his trial as an opportunity to declare the Gospel to Caesar and his
court, and through this **heralding** and proclamation **all the Gentiles**
heard his message. Thus he was granted a stay of immediate execution and another hearing, so that he **was rescued out of the lion's
mouth**. (It is possible that the reference to the lion's mouth might
not be merely metaphorical, but may refer to Paul's being thrown
to the lions, as many Christians were under Nero. This would then

mean that at his trial Paul established his right as a Roman citizen to be exempt from such punishment.)

St. Paul knows that the Lord is faithful (even if his Roman friends are not). As He rescued him at his first hearing, so He will **rescue** him **from every evil work** that his foes plan. Paul will not apostatize, whatever his adversaries hope, but will by God's grace persevere to the end. Thus will Christ **save** him and bring him **to His heavenly Kingdom**. (The verb used is *sozo*, the usual word for "to save"; its use here shows that salvation is not complete until we finally enter the Kingdom.) Paul takes no credit for himself. On the contrary, as a good Jew, he ascribes all the **glory** to God, even **to the ages of the ages**.

ॐ ॐ ॐ ॐ ॐ

19 Greet Prisca and Aquila and the house of Onesiphorus.

20 Erastus remained at Corinth, but Trophimus I left ailing in Miletus.

21 Be diligent to come before winter. Eubulus greets you; and *so do* Pudens and Linus and Claudia and all the brothers.

As was usual in such epistles, Paul adds a series of greetings. Timothy is to greet Paul's old co-workers, the husband-and-wife team of **Prisca and Aquila**. Of the two, it would seem the wife Prisca was the more dominant, since she is often mentioned before her husband (see Acts 18:18, 26; Rom. 16:3). Timothy is also to greet **the house of Onesiphorus**, who had died (as we suggested above in comments on 1:16), and to whose surviving family the apostle now sends greetings.

There is more news. **Erastus remained at Corinth**, where he was (probably) the city treasurer (Rom. 16:23) and where Paul left him after passing through that city, as Erastus declined to accompany Paul further on his travels. **Trophimus** (the cause of Paul's first arrest in the Jerusalem temple; see Acts 21:29) was **left ailing** and unable to travel **in Miletus**, near Ephesus. (Possibly Paul traveled through Miletus after his arrest in Ephesus on his way to Rome.) Whatever the specific circumstances, Timothy should not hope to find these men in Rome when he arrives there, contrary perhaps to what he may expect.

Paul passes on the greetings of those who are in Rome. **Eubulus** (otherwise unknown in the NT) greets Timothy, as do **Pudens** and **Claudia**. Some have thought that Pudens and Claudia were husband and wife, though the presence of the name of Linus between theirs argues against this. Researchers have found the name Pudens listed on an old Roman inscription as a servant of Emperor Claudius, and this may be the man mentioned here. **Linus** is almost certainly the one mentioned by Irenaeus (in his *Against Heresies* 3.3) as the bishop of Rome, next in succession from Peter. **All the brothers** are doubtless all the local faithful of the Roman Church.

§IX. Concluding Blessing (4:22)

> ৩৯ ৩৯ ৩৯ ৩৯ ৩৯
>
> **22 The Lord *be* with your spirit. Grace *be* with you.**

St. Paul then concludes his epistle with his customary apostolic blessing. He prays **the Lord's** presence and all His mercy on Timothy's **spirit**, to strengthen him in his innermost being. He also prays God's **grace** on all who may read the epistle (the **you** is plural). It is fitting that the last written and extant words of the great apostle are words of grace. After writing this epistle, he put down his pen and, strengthened by his friends and the Lord's grace, walked the last few miles into the Kingdom.

By common reckoning, in late June (perhaps in the year 66), the former persecutor of the Church was taken to a place outside the city walls, on the road to Ostia, the city port. There he laid aside his garments in preparation for beheading and knelt down, surrendering his neck to the Roman sword and his soul to his heavenly Master. The former persecutor had become the great apostle to the Gentiles, had stood before Gentiles and kings for the sake of Christ (cf. Acts 9:15), and had filled the world with his teaching. Now was the time for his final reward and for a weight of glory. The executioner's stroke released him from his labors and sent him to be with his Lord. For him, to live was Christ and to die was gain (Phil. 1:21), and he remains in the Church as foremost in the ranks of the apostles and as a teacher of the world. Through his holy prayers, Lord Jesus Christ our God, have mercy on us!

About the Author

Archpriest Lawrence Farley currently pastors St. Herman of Alaska Orthodox Church (OCA) in Langley, B.C., Canada. He received his B.A. from Trinity College, Toronto, and his M.Div. from Wycliffe College, Toronto. A former Anglican priest, he converted to Orthodoxy in 1985 and studied for two years at St. Tikhon's Orthodox Seminary in Pennsylvania. In addition to the books in the Orthodox Bible Study Companion series, he has also published *The Christian Old Testament: Looking at the Hebrew Scriptures through Christian Eyes; A Song in the Furnace: The Message of the Book of Daniel; Unquenchable Fire: The Traditional Christian Teaching about Hell; A Daily Calendar of Saints: A Synaxarion for Today's North American Church; Let Us Attend: A Journey Through the Orthodox Divine Liturgy; One Flesh: Salvation through Marriage in the Orthodox Church; The Empty Throne: Reflections on the History and Future of the Orthodox Episcopacy;* and *Following Egeria: A Visit to the Holy Land through Time and Space.*

Visit www.ancientfaithradio.com to listen to Fr. Lawrence Farley's regular podcast, "No Other Foundation: Reflections on Orthodox Theology and Biblical Studies."

A Complete List of the Books in the Orthodox Bible Study Companion Series

The Gospel of Matthew
Torah for the Church
• Paperback, 400 pages, ISBN 978-0-9822770-7-2

The Gospel of Mark
The Suffering Servant
• Paperback, 280 pages, ISBN 978-1-888212-54-9

The Gospel of Luke
Good News for the Poor
• Paperback, 432 pages, ISBN 978-1-936270-12-5

The Gospel of John
Beholding the Glory
• Paperback, 376 pages, ISBN 978-1-888212-55-6

The Acts of the Apostles
Spreading the Word
• Paperback, 352 pages, ISBN 978-1-936270-62-0

The Epistle to the Romans
A Gospel for All
• Paperback, 208 pages, ISBN 978-1-888212-51-8

First and Second Corinthians
Straight from the Heart
• Paperback, 319 pages, ISBN 978-1-888212-53-2

Words of Fire
The Early Epistles of St. Paul to the Thessalonians and the Galatians
• Paperback, 172 pages, ISBN 978-1-936270-02-6

The Prison Epistles
Philippians – Ephesians – Colossians – Philemon
• Paperback, 224 pages, ISBN 978-1-888212-52-5

Shepherding the Flock
The Pastoral Epistles of St. Paul the Apostle to Timothy and Titus
• Paperback, 144 pages, ISBN 978-1-888212-56-3

The Epistle to the Hebrews
High Priest in Heaven
• Paperback, 184 pages, ISBN 978-1-936270-74-3

Universal Truth
The Catholic Epistles of James, Peter, Jude, and John
• Paperback, 232 pages, ISBN 978-1-888212-60-0

The Apocalypse of St. John
A Revelation of Love and Power
• Paperback, 240 pages, ISBN 978-1-936270-40-8

Other Books by the Author

The Christian Old Testament
Looking at the Hebrew Scriptures through Christian Eyes
Many Christians see the Old Testament as "the other Testament": a source of exciting stories to tell the kids, but not very relevant to the Christian life. *The Christian Old Testament* reveals the Hebrew Scriptures as the essential context of Christianity, as well as a many-layered revelation of Christ Himself. Follow along as Fr. Lawrence Farley explores the Christian significance of every book of the Old Testament.
• Paperback, 200 pages, ISBN 978-1-936270-53-8

A Song in the Furnace
The Message of the Book of Daniel
The Book of Daniel should be read with the eyes of a child. It's a book of wonders and extremes—mad kings, baffling dreams with gifted interpreters, breathtaking deliverances, astounding prophecies—with even what may be the world's first detective stories added in for good measure. To argue over the book's historicity, as scholars have done for centuries, is to miss the point. In *A Song in the Furnace*, Fr. Lawrence Farley reveals all the wonders of this unique book to the receptive eye.
• Paperback, 248 pages, ISBN 978-1-944967-31-4

A Daily Calendar of Saints
A Synaxarion for Today's North American Church
Popular biblical commentator and church historian Fr. Lawrence Farley turns his hand to hagiography in this collection of lives of saints, one or more for each day of the calendar year. His accessible prose and contemporary approach make these ancient lives easy for modern Christians to relate to and understand.
• Paperback, 304 pages, ISBN 978-1-944967-41-3

Unquenchable Fire
The Traditional Christian Teaching about Hell

The doctrine of hell as a place of eternal punishment has never been easy for Christians to accept. The temptation to retreat from and reject the Church's traditional teaching about hell is particularly strong in our current culture, which has demonstrably lost its sense of sin. Fr. Lawrence Farley examines the Orthodox Church's teaching on this difficult subject through the lens of Scripture and patristic writings, making the case that the existence of hell does not negate that of a loving and forgiving God.

• Paperback, 240 pages, ISBN 978-1-944967-18-5

Let Us Attend
A Journey Through the Orthodox Divine Liturgy

Fr. Lawrence Farley provides a guide to understanding the Divine Liturgy, and a vibrant reminder of the centrality of the Eucharist in living the Christian life, guiding believers in a devotional and historical walk through the Orthodox Liturgy. Examining the Liturgy section by section, he provides both historical explanations of how the Liturgy evolved and devotional insights aimed at helping us pray the Liturgy in the way the Fathers intended.

• Paperback, 104 pages, ISBN 978-1-888212-87-7

One Flesh
Salvation through Marriage in the Orthodox Church

Is the Church too negative about sex? Beginning with this provocative question, Fr. Lawrence Farley explores the history of the Church's attitude toward sex and marriage, from the Old Testament through the Church Fathers. He persuasively makes the case both for traditional morality and for a positive acceptance of marriage as a viable path to theosis.

• Paperback, 160 pages, ISBN 978-1-936270-66-8

The Empty Throne
Reflections on the History and Future of the Orthodox Episcopacy

In contemporary North America, the bishop's throne in the local parish stands empty for most of the year. The bishop is an honored occasional guest rather than a true pastor of the local flock. But it was not always so, nor need it be so forever. Fr. Lawrence Farley explores how the Orthodox episcopacy developed over the centuries and suggests what can be done in modern times to bring the bishop back into closer contact with his flock.

• Paperback, 152 pages, ISBN 978-1-936270-61-3

Following Egeria
A Visit to the Holy Land through Time and Space

In the fourth century, a nun named Egeria traveled through the Holy Land and wrote an account of her experiences. In the twenty-first century, Fr. Lawrence

Farley followed partially in her footsteps and wrote his own account of how he experienced the holy sites as they are today. Whether you're planning your own pilgrimage or want to read about places you may never go, his account will inform and inspire you.

• Paperback, 160 pages, ISBN 978-1-936270-21-7

Three Akathists:

Akathist to Jesus, Light to Those in Darkness

• Staple-bound, 32 pages, ISBN 978-1-944967-33-8

Akathist to the Most Holy Theotokos, Daughter of Zion

• Staple-bound, 32 pages, ISBN 978-1-944967-34-4

Akathist to Matushka Olga Michael

• Staple-bound, 32 pages, ISBN 978-1-944967-38-3

For complete ordering information, visit our website: store.ancientfaith.com.

We hope you have enjoyed and benefited from this book. Your financial support makes it possible to continue our nonprofit ministry both in print and online. Because the proceeds from our book sales only partially cover the costs of operating **Ancient Faith Publishing** and **Ancient Faith Radio**, we greatly appreciate the generosity of our readers and listeners. Donations are tax deductible and can be made at **www.ancientfaith.com**.

To view our other publications,
please visit our website: **store.ancientfaith.com**

 **ANCIENT FAITH RADIO**

Bringing you Orthodox Christian music, readings,
prayers, teaching, and podcasts 24 hours a day since 2004 at
www.ancientfaith.com